FAITH
IMPROVISA
CW00816226

About the Editors

The Revd Canon Professor **Loveday Alexander** is Emeritus Professor of Biblical Studies at the University of Sheffield, Emeritus Canon-Theologian at Chester Cathedral, and a member of the Faith and Order Commission. Her publications focus on the interfaces between the Bible, the classical world, and the Church.

Professor **Mike Higton** is Professor of Theology and Ministry at Durham University and a member of the Faith and Order Commission. He oversees the 'Common Awards' partnership with Durham University, which validates much of the ministerial training of the Church of England and the Methodist Church of Great Britain.

About the Contributors

The Revd Dr **Cally [Carolyn] Hammond** is Dean of Gonville and Caius College, Cambridge, and was a member of the Faith and Order Commission until 2016. She writes on early Christian literature (including a new translation of the Confessions of St Augustine), and on prayer and the language of liturgy.

Tim Harle is Programme Leader for Sarum College's MA in Christian Approaches to Leadership. He undertook Advanced Management Studies at INSEAD and is a Visiting Fellow at Bristol Business School. Tim's publications include contributions to *Moving on in Ministry* (CHP, 2013) and *Developing Leadership* (Sage, 2015). You can follow him @*TimHarle*.

The Revd **Dr David Hilborn** is Principal of St John's School of Mission, Nottingham, and was a member of the Faith and Order Commission until 2016. He was previously Assistant Dean of St Mellitus College and Head of Theology at the Evangelical Alliance. He writes on the history of Evangelicalism.

The Revd Canon **Dr Charlotte Methuen** is Senior Lecturer in Church History at the University of Glasgow with a particular interest in the Reformation and in the history of orders. She is a member of IASCUFO [the Inter-Anglican Standing Committee on Unity, Faith and Order] and served on the Faith and Order Commission and its predecessor until 2016.

The Revd **Dr Jeremy Morris** is Master of Trinity Hall, Cambridge. He is a modern church historian and served on the Faith and Order Commission and its predecessor until 2016.

Father **Thomas Sevile** CR is a monk of the Community of the Resurrection, a member of the Faith and Order Commission and a tutor of the College of the Resurrection, Mirfield.

The **Rt Revd Rachel Treweek** is Bishop of Gloucester.

FAITHFUL IMPROVISATION?

Theological Reflections on Church Leadership

edited by

Loveday Alexander and Mike Higton

Including the report from the Church of England's Faith and Order Commission on Senior Church Leadership

Faithful Improvisation?
Theological Reflections on Church Leadership

Edited by Loveday Alexander and Mike Higton

Including the report from the
Church of England's Faith and Order Commission
on Senior Church Leadership

Church House Publishing
Church House
Great Smith Street
London
SW1P 3AZ

ISBN: 978 0 7151 4738 2

Published in 2016 by Church House Publishing

Only the Faith and Order Commission report *Senior Church Leadership: A Resource for Reflection* (Part 1 of this volume) has the authority of the Commission that approved it.

The opinions expressed in the remainder of this book are those of the editors and contributors and do not necessarily reflect the official policy of the General Synod or the Archbishops' Council of the Church of England.

British Library Cataloguing in Publication data

A catalogue record for this book is available
from the British Library

Printed and bound in Great Britain by CPI Group (UK) Ltd, Croydon

Contents

Introduction

Church bodies are constantly producing reports. The fact that they can now be distributed and accessed electronically has only encouraged the flow. Most are only intended for a limited audience, and usually address a specific set of circumstances. The enduring significance in many cases will be primarily in how they contribute to a wider story around the church's handling of a particular issue, rather than as freestanding works.

Senior Church Leadership: A Resource for Reflection is a report from a church body, the Church of England's Faith and Order Commission, but unlike many such reports it was always intended to be a document of wide interest in its own right within and beyond the Church of England, and to be a substantial text on a pivotal issue for church life in the contemporary world that could continue to be read with profit many years after its initial publication. I am therefore delighted, as chair of the Faith and Order Commission, that it is being published in book form by Church House Publishing, together with some of the more detailed background work that informed it and some brief reflections on how it is being received in the life of the church. The book as a whole deserves to be widely read and to become a standard item on bibliographies for courses on church leadership at every level – and indeed to attract interest from students of leadership studies as a secular discipline.

Since publication, the *Senior Church Leadership* report has received considerable attention within the Church of England, including extended discussion in the College of Bishops. Much appreciation was expressed during the debate about it at General Synod in July 2015, which featured a number of very thoughtful and constructive contributions, including a speech from the Archbishop of Canterbury. As he perceptively commented, 'The question the report addresses is how leadership is continually redefined into a model that is truly Christ-like.' The Archbishop then proceeded to say that

> The FAOC report shows that leadership needs preparation in prayer, in theology, in the skills of everyday matters, in collaborative working, in interpreting the times, in safeguarding, in how to ensure overall that what the Church discerns as necessary the Church does. We must have a system that is pastorally sensitive for those being formed, self-consciously inclusive of those we too easily exclude, and ensures that those being considered for appointments in posts of wide responsibility are from all areas of the Church and are diverse ... Our theology and practice must challenge inherited or widely accepted bad models through prayer and also theological thinking.

I am grateful to the Archbishop for pointing out so clearly the relevance of the report for how the church approaches the task of preparing people for positions of leadership. The Church of England has seen some vigorous and impassioned exchanges on this subject since a pre-publication version of the Report of the Lord Green Steering Group, *Talent Management for Future Leaders and Leadership Development for Bishops and Deans: A New Approach*, came into the public domain in December 2014. Indeed, the Synod debate in July 2014 almost inevitably encompassed comments on that document and on the major new programmes of leadership development that were initiated in its wake. These programmes are still at a very early stage, with some shorter courses having run once or twice only, while with longer programmes it will be several years before a complete first cycle will have taken place. Initial feedback from participants, however, has been encouraging, and my hope is that *Senior Church Leadership* will become a valuable resource for them and for those with responsibility for education and formation in this area. The word 'resource' is important here; the Faith and Order Commission had no intention of writing a textbook, and the intelligent criticism of some aspects of the report in the Synod debate, for instance, represents just the kind of rigorous theological thinking about leadership to which we hoped it would contribute.

The book is divided into three parts, and it will be helpful to be aware of the significant differences between them. Part 1 contains the Faith and Order Commission's report, *Senior Church Leadership*. Of course, this reflects the perspectives of individual members of the Commission at various points, but it is a document of the Commission and the Commission alone is responsible for its contents. The other two parts of the book are quite different, in that they contain articles by various authors writing in their personal capacity. Thus while most (though not all) of the authors are members of the Commission, their contributions to Parts 2 and 3 represent their own views and do not come with any kind of imprimatur from it.

Following the text of the report itself, Part 2 of the book presents in more detail work that fed into the deliberations of the Commission from which *Senior Church Leadership* emerged. The five essays assembled here, by Cally Hammond, Thomas Seville, Charlotte Methuen, Jeremy Morris, and David Hilborn, examine practices, models and theologies of leadership in relation to different periods of church history. In Part 3, the perspective shifts to take in the broader discussion about leadership within the Church of England since the on-line publication of the Commission's report. Here, Mike Higton sketches out a dialogue between *Senior Church Leadership* and *Talent Management for Future Leaders*; Tim Harle offers a personal reflection from the perspective of the community of leadership practitioners; and Rachel Treweek, still in her early days as Bishop of Gloucester at the time of writing, generously provides a concluding reflection (based on her contribution to the discussion at the College of Bishops meeting in September 2015), for which I am especially grateful. The Commission has been much helped by those who have acted as external consultants and sounding boards at various stages of discussion along the way, notably Paul Avis, Keith Lamdin, Tim Ling, and Tim Harle, and I am very grateful for the way they have enriched our thinking and enhanced our writing.

Finally, may I emphasise that this book and the report it contains are intended to be a resource not just for discussions about leadership, in synods or in classrooms, but for doing the work of leadership in the life of the church in such a way that it can, as Archbishop Justin said, be 'continually redefined into a model that is truly Christ-like.' That means readers will need to relate it to the opportunities and challenges of leadership that they face in their particular contexts. In my own case, I have been encouraged to reflect on how leadership relates to the distinctive charisms of episcopal ministry, beginning with that 'overseeing' which involves seeing beyond the immediate and the proximate. Such seeing is bound to suffering, sharing the pains of parishes and communities that are going through difficult times, and also, partly as a consequence, carries a responsibility for strategic missionary thought and action, listening to what the Spirit is saying to the churches and then acting upon it. All of this is held together by love: love is at the heart of the charism of the bishop, as it is in any form of Christian leadership, and any form of education in church leadership needs to hold love, and the renewal of love, at the centre.

The Preface to Senior Church Leadership notes the debt the Faith and Order Commission owes to Professors Loveday Alexander and Mike Higton for their role in drafting that text. That debt has now become weightier with the work they have done as editors, in assembling the contributions in Part 2 and Part 3 and bringing this volume to publication. The Faith and Order Commission, the church body that produced the report in Part 1, is appointed for a five-year period, and this project was never far from its focus throughout its term from 2010 to 2015. I would therefore also like to record my gratitude to all the members of the Commission for their various contributions to the thinking about leadership conveyed in this book, which can stand as an enduring testimony to their dedicated service to the Church of England.

The Right Reverend Dr Christopher Cocksworth

The Bishop of Coventry

Part 1

The FAOC report

Senior Church Leadership: A Resource for Reflection

Preface

The following report from the Faith and Order Commission of the Church of England originated from a motion passed at the General Synod in 2009. The motion asked for a report '(i) bringing together existing material in the Church of England and the Anglican Communion relating to the exercise of senior leadership in the Church; and (ii) setting out biblical and theological perspectives to inform the Church's developing patterns of senior leadership'.[1] Inevitably, the material has evolved in significant ways while the Commission has been working on it over the past five years.

During that time, leadership has remained a crucial area of concern within and beyond the Church of England. It has continued to provoke sharp debates among Christians, often focusing on how best to engage with a perceived 'secular' discourse for understanding and developing the ministry of the church. This was evident most recently in some of the initial reactions to the Report of the Lord Green Steering Group, *Talent Management for Future Leaders and Leadership Development for Bishops and Deans: A New Approach,* released in December 2014.

For reasons that are set out in chapter 2 of our report, it is necessary for the Church of England to respond to particular challenges around leadership, facing all the practical demands that this involves. Our intention, however, is not to make recommendations about how the church should act with regard to specific issues. Nor is it to set out some kind of formal doctrinal position. It is certainly not to provide a leadership manual. Rather, we have understood our task as being to produce a 'resource for reflection', as chapter 1 explains – one that can inform the improvisations that the church will continue to require in its practice of leadership and anchor them in faithfulness to the gospel.

1 See https://www.churchofengland.org/media-centre/news/2009/07/gsjul120709.aspx.

What follows embodies the kind of careful dialogue we aim to promote between theological and 'organisational' ways of thinking. How do the dynamics of church life and leadership in the New Testament apply to the church today? How might we draw faithfully and creatively on the rich traditions of the church over two millennia concerning authority, responsibility and service? How can we talk constructively about ambition in church life and deal with the realities of disappointment and the experience of failure? These are not just issues for those who exercise senior leadership in the Church of England, and we hope that this report can contribute to fostering serious thought and prayer about them.

A report such as this is indebted to many people working together over an extended period of time, and the current Commission as a whole is responsible for its final content. That said, I would especially like to thank Professor Loveday Alexander and Professor Mike Higton, who have given very generously of their time, knowledge and skill to draft the report and bring it to completion.

The Faith and Order Commission is glad to offer this report as 'a resource for reflection' in the hope that it may serve the church's understanding of itself and the leadership that it requires today.

CHRISTOPHER COVENTRY

Chair, Faith and Order Commission

Introduction

1 At times, it can seem as if everyone in the church is talking about leaders and leadership. There are, for instance, tens of thousands of examples on the internet of people saying 'the church needs leaders who ...'. Type the phrase into a search engine, and you will quickly find people saying that the church needs leaders

- who are bold and alert,
- who can energise people,
- who can cherish and communicate vision,
- who have the skills to lead people through transition and change, and
- who can ensure that we hand the church to the next generation in better shape than we found it.

You will just as quickly find people saying that the church needs leaders

- who are biblically literate and faithfully orthodox,
- who are compelled to minister out of love for God's Word,
- who know their purpose in Christ,
- who have a personal relationship with God, and
- who live out gospel values.

2 This talk about leadership in the church is very varied. Much of it expresses a need or desire for leadership, for the sake of the flourishing of the church's ministry and mission – though there are many different accounts of the kind of leadership that will lead to flourishing, and many different accounts of the kind of flourishing hoped for.

3 Much of the talk is about the qualities or characteristics that leaders will need if they are to be faithful leaders, deeply rooted in the faith – though here again there are many different accounts of the nature of that rooting, and many different descriptions of the ways in which we can expect it to be displayed.

4 There is also, however, a good deal of talk that comments critically on all these proposals for leadership, and expresses concern at the very fact that talk about leadership has come to be so prominent in the life of the church – though here, too, there are many different forms of criticism offered, on many different grounds.

5 This widespread and varied talk forms the background against which we have written this report.

1.1 Questions about senior leadership

6 We had a particular remit to focus on senior leadership in the Church of England. 'Senior leadership' is not itself a category that is used in formal documents from the Church of England,[1] but for our purposes we have taken the term to refer to those who exercise some kind of ministry of oversight (that is, *episkope*) that extends beyond a particular congregation, especially when it extends regionally or nationally. We have focused most directly on the leadership provided by bishops, but we have tried at various points, and especially in the central biblical exploration, to set that focus against a wider background.

---

2 Unlike the Methodist Church, for instance, which uses the term 'senior leadership group' under 'Connexional team' at http://methodist.org.uk

7 Our intention to focus on 'senior leadership' arose in response to a cluster of concerns that have surfaced repeatedly in recent years. These have included:

- tensions between legal accounts of church governance that focus on the office of the diocesan bishop in relative isolation, and the collaborative practice of leadership in dioceses by senior staff teams;
- tensions between accounts that focus on the diocesan bishop in relative isolation, and the collegial practice of leadership at national level through the College and House of Bishops;
- questions about the relationship between the leadership of the church by its bishops and the institutional management of the church by its central administration;
- questions about the roles played in cathedrals, dioceses and the national church by senior lay people in key positions, and the need for both recognition and reflection in this area;
- questions about the role of suffragan bishops, about the role of archdeacons and about the relationships between the two, and a lack of consistency between dioceses in the understanding of these roles;
- questions about the processes by which the Church of England encourages, identifies and prepares men and women for senior clergy appointments, and supports them appropriately while in post; and
- questions about the teaching role of the bishops and about the best means to support and develop it.

8 Those specific issues are, however, surrounded by more general questions sparked by the term 'leadership' itself.

- What is the relationship between the leadership of individuals and leadership distributed across an institution? Are leaders there to do the leading themselves, or do they enable leadership to emerge at various levels?
- Is leadership always collaborative, and if so who are the partners? To what extent does such partnership need to be expressed in role descriptions and formal frameworks as well as in informal commitments and good intentions?
- Where, in a collaborative and collegial vision of ministry and mission, is there room for prophetic and critical leadership, and for individual accountability and responsibility?
- To what extent are wisdom and expertise about senior leadership from other institutions (businesses, the public sector, academic research) directly transferable to the life of the Church of England?
- To what extent can the church's wisdom and expertise about senior leadership be useful in other organisations and institutions in the world?
- Can the church be honest, transparent and rigorous in seeking to nurture the senior leadership it needs while giving proper 'honour' to every member of the body (1 Corinthians 12.12–31), and without discouraging those whose calling is in other spheres?

9 The main questions that faced us as we began our work were therefore:

- Is it right to make 'leadership' a central idea in the life of the church?
- If so, what are the underlying *theological* principles that inform the exercise of leadership within the church?
- How can these principles best inform the exercise of senior leadership in the Church of England today?

1.2 The purpose of this report

10 In Section 2 of this report, we will examine both the rise of leadership language in the life of the church and some of the criticisms that have been made of it. We recognise that this language is not going away any time soon. It has simply become too prevalent and too deeply embedded, and we acknowledge that this is in part because it can name important needs in the church's life. Rather than arguing about whether we should stop using leadership language, therefore, we discuss how this language might be used well, and how the dangers involved can be recognised and avoided. Our initial, provisional answer to the first question ('Is it right to make "leadership" a central idea in the life of the church?') is therefore: 'It is unavoidable – but we should treat it with caution.'

11 For the second question ('If so, what are the underlying theological principles that inform the exercise of leadership within the church?') we turn to the church's traditional resources of 'Scripture, tradition and reason'. That is, we seek to shape our understanding of leadership by means of a reasoned engagement with Scripture, in conversation with the ongoing Christian tradition. In Section 3, we explore the practice of leadership in the New Testament – not because such a study can provide a simple blueprint for our practice today, nor because it can answer all the questions we might have, but because it witnesses to the deepest demands to which all attempts at faithful Christian leadership must respond. In Section 4 we offer a necessarily brief description of some of the ways in which Christians have responded to those demands through the history of the church, constantly adopting and adapting the practices of leadership they inherited from previous generations in the light of their changing context. In Section 5 we draw out a series of lessons for the contemporary exercise of leadership (especially senior leadership) in the church today.

12 We do not claim, however, to provide a detailed answer to the third question, 'How can these principles best inform the exercise of senior leadership in the Church of England today?' That is because compelling answers to that question are not developed in the pages of reports. They are developed *in situ*, hammered out in context by Christians drawing deeply on the Scriptures, engaging with the tradition, attending to their situations, questioning and challenging and encouraging one another, and discovering prayerfully over time what bears fruit and what does not.

13 In other words, good answers to this question are produced by *faithful improvisation*, in the never-ending diversity of contexts in which the church finds itself. By 'improvisation', we do not mean 'making it up as we go along' or 'bodging something together from the materials available'. Rather, we are drawing on the way that 'improvisation' has been written about by a number of theologians in recent years,[3] and are using the word in something like the sense it can have in musical performance. Musicians who are deeply trained in a particular tradition (who know its constraints and possibilities in their bones) draw on all the resources provided by that formation to respond creatively to new situations and to one another. Compelling and faithful answers to the church's questions about leadership require something of the same deep formation and deep attentiveness *in situ*, and will be similarly diverse and creative.

14 A brief report from an official Commission, speaking about senior leadership across the whole Church of England, cannot provide a shortcut through that process. We have not, therefore, tried to provide detailed practical recommendations about the shape that senior leadership should take in today's church, nor

---

3 See, for instance, Jeremy Begbie, *Theology, Music and Time*, Cambridge: Cambridge University Press, 2000; Kevin J. Vanhoozer, *The Drama of Doctrine: A Canonical-Linguistic Approach to Christian Theology*, Louisville, KY: Westminster John Knox, 2005; Samuel Wells, *Improvisation: The Drama of Christian Ethics*, London: SPCK, 2004; and Frances Young, *The Art of Performance: Towards a Theology of Holy Scripture*, London: Darton, Longman and Todd, 1990.

about the ways in which the challenges facing senior leaders should be tackled. What we have tried to produce, instead, is a 'resource for reflection': a prompt to those who are involved in the real process of answering that question in their own situation, that will help stimulate the improvisation that is needed and help clarify some of the questions we should ask as we try to keep those improvisations faithful.

15 It is our hope that the report as a whole will encourage those involved in the process of faithful improvisation, and help them to hear some of the questions they can and should be asking as they go about their task.

2 For and against 'leadership'

16 Recently, the need for leadership in the church has been in the news again, thanks to the findings of the Church Growth Research Programme. In a Church of England press release, Professor David Voas, one of the leaders of the research, said that 'Growth is a product of good leadership (lay and ordained) working with a willing set of churchgoers in a favourable environment'.[4] In the same press release, 'leadership' tops the list of 'common ingredients strongly associated with growth', a list that also includes 'clear mission and purpose', 'being intentional' and 'vision'. The Programme's report, *From Anecdote to Evidence: Findings from the Church Growth Research Programme 2011–2013*,[5] makes it clear that the 'leadership' in question is a matter of 'motivating people, inspiring and generating enthusiasm to action' (p. 8); that is what they have discovered is needed for growth.

---

4 Church of England Press Office, 'Signs of Growth: Cathedrals, Fresh Expressions, and Parishes around the Country Provide Grounds for Growth of Church of England', 16 January 2014, https://www.churchofengland.org/media-centre/news/2014/01/signs-of-growth.aspx.

5 Church Growth Research Programme, 2014, http://www.churchgrowthresearch.org.uk/UserFiles/File/Reports/FromAnecdoteToEvidence1.0.pdf.

17 This is only the latest episode in a history of increasing attention to leadership in the church over the past half-century. Although talk about leadership was not much in evidence in the Church of England in the nineteenth century or the first half of the twentieth, it began to emerge after the Second World War. It became noticeably more prominent in the 1960s (perhaps not coincidentally a decade in which there was a sharp decline in church attendance), and then really took off in the 1980s. That rise to prominence has, however, been accompanied by a chorus of questions about the appropriateness of a focus on leadership in the life of the church.

2.1 The rise of leadership

18 A marker of things to come can be found in the translation of 1 Timothy 3.1–2 in the New English Bible, published in 1961. Where the RSV had spoken about bishops and those who aspire 'to the office of a bishop', the NEB speaks about 'our *leader* or bishop' and those who aspire 'to leadership'.

19 Nearly two decades later, in 1980, the language of leadership appeared in the *Alternative Service Book* ordinal. Using a term that does not appear in the *Book of Common Prayer* equivalent, it says that the ordained minister 'is to lead his people in prayer and worship'. There is no reference to this choice of word in the notes from the revision process, but that the word was increasingly 'in the air' in relation to ministry is demonstrated by the fact that, two years later, the major ecumenical report *Baptism, Eucharist and Ministry* could speak of ordained ministers 'called to exercise wise and loving leadership' (Ministry, §16), and of bishops having 'responsibility for leadership in the Church's mission' (§29).[6] As a term without

6 *Baptism, Eucharist and Ministry*, Faith and Order Paper 111, Geneva: World Council of Churches, 1982,, http://www.oikoumene.org/en/resources/documents/wcc-commissions/faith-and-order-commission/i-unity-the-church-and-its-mission/baptism-eucharist-and-ministry-faith-and-order-paper-no-111-the-lima-text.

obvious denominational baggage, its prominence in an ecumenical context should probably not surprise us.

20 Over the next decade and a half, talk of leadership became an essential part of discussions of ordained ministry in the Church of England.[7] In 1993, the Working Party on Criteria for Selection for Ministry in the Church of England introduced 'Leadership and Collaboration' to those criteria, and said that 'A basic ability required of leaders is to identify where the group or community stands and what it should aim to achieve. Leaders should then be able to set out the means to obtain the objectives, drawing the group or community towards the aim and motivating its members towards the goal' (§96). 'This ability includes the capacity to offer an example of faith and discipleship, to collaborate effectively with others, as well as to guide and shape the life of the Church community in its mission to the world' (§102).

21 Two years later, in *Working as One Body: The Report of the Archbishops' Commission on the Organisation of the Church of England* (1995), the language of leadership was used prominently to describe the role of bishops.[8] The church 'combines leadership by bishops with governance by synods representing bishops, clergy, laity', and such leadership is 'essentially the enablement of life and work in the dioceses' (§1.1). This is possible in part because 'God has given outstanding skills of leadership to particular individuals' (§1.24).

22 Over the same period, leadership language has become increasingly common in evangelical churches, intentional communities, networks and agencies, where again its lack of

---

7 *The Report of a Working Party on Criteria for Selection for Ministry in the Church of England*, ABM Policy Paper No. 3A (1993).

8 Working as One Body: The Report of the Archbishops' Commission on the Organisation of the Church of England, London: Church House, 1995.

denominational and traditional baggage has made it very useful. Its usage was cemented by events like the Evangelical Alliance's Leadership '84 conference, a gathering of some 1,500 Christian leaders.[9]

23 By the time that Steven Croft wrote *Ministry in Three Dimensions: Ordination and Leadership in the Local Church* in 1999, he was able to say that in a wide variety of church contexts 'leader' was becoming 'the most commonly used title for a person called to full-time Christian work' and that, 'if anything, leadership language is becoming even more predominant across the traditions'.[10]

2.2 The desire for leadership

24 A full analysis of the rise of leadership language in recent decades would take many pages and would take us well beyond our remit here. Nevertheless, it is possible to identify several themes that come up repeatedly when Christians talk about leadership in relation to the church's ministry and mission.

25 There is a widespread desire for leaders who can inspire, encourage and sustain the people of God in their collective ministry and mission: leaders with a compelling vision for the growth and flourishing of the church. Sometimes calls for more and better leadership are framed by descriptions of the church as a flock without a shepherd. Those looking for leadership ask where we will find the shepherds of the people, capable of gathering God's people into the life and work that God has for them, and facing up to the urgent needs of the church in the world.

---

9 See below, §§158–160.

10 Stephen Croft, *Ministry in Three Dimensions*, London: DLT, 1999. p. 203, n. 26.

26 There is a widespread desire for leaders who can animate and inspire the church's worship of God. One sign of this desire is the increasing prevalence of the term 'worship leader', though the desire for leadership in worship stretches wider than that. There are calls for leaders who can preside over the people's worship, keeping God at the centre of the church's focus and finding new ways in which that focus can be made palpable in every aspect of the church's life.

27 There is a widespread desire for leaders capable of compelling teaching. Often calls for more or better leadership in the church are framed by a description of the uncertainty of the church's voice, and by the contrast between that uncertainty and the great prophetic and teaching voices of the tradition. Those looking for leadership ask where that bold and captivating speech is to be found in today's church.

28 There is a widespread desire for leaders who can engage confidently and persuasively with the wider world. Descriptions of the church's uncertain voice often focus on the failures of its communication with the wider world: the lack of evangelistic passion, the lack of compelling apologetic, the lack of moral leadership, the failure to speak truth to power. Those looking for more and better leadership in the church are often asking for those who will be capable of speaking powerfully on the church's behalf in the world, and of working transformatively with others in the world.

29 There is a widespread desire for leaders who will take absolutely seriously their personal and public accountability, especially in relation to issues of abuse and safeguarding. Leaders – especially diocesan bishops – have to acknowledge that the buck stops with them and that their responsibility cannot be fudged or avoided.

30 Finally there is also, and perhaps most fundamentally, a widespread desire for leaders who can respond creatively to change. Statements of the need for good leadership in the church are often framed by descriptions of the huge changes affecting the church and its position in society: changes in size, importance, activity, culture, image, legislation and diversity. And they are often framed by an account of the need and opportunity for mission that those changes create. Those looking for renewed church leadership are often looking for leaders who will help the church respond creatively to all these changes so as to flourish in the new contexts that they create, and who will be capable of taking the church deeper into mission.

31 Each of these desires can be framed in many different ways. The visions of the church's ministry and mission that animate these hopes vary widely, as do the relative emphases placed on each of these elements. Any attempt to give more practical detail to these rather generalised descriptions of what leadership might mean would immediately invite debate, some of it fierce, and even the little we have already said no doubt rings truer to some readers than to others.

32 Nevertheless, one central point is emerging, and it is one to which we will be returning several times in this report. Our questions about leadership need to be asked in relation to the ministry and mission of the church, the ministry and mission given to it by God. We cannot hold a meaningful conversation about 'leadership' in isolation from the urgent and necessary conversations taking place within the church about the mission and ministry of the whole people of God.

2.3 The problems with leadership

33 The rise and rise of the language of leadership in the Church of England has generated a family of serious concerns.

2.3.1 The language of leadership

34 We will be discussing in more detail below the fact that the use of leadership language to talk about Christ's church is not particularly biblical – and the fact that this is not itself necessarily a problem (since the church is always unavoidably involved in borrowing and transforming language from elsewhere). Nevertheless, it is a telling fact that the New Testament authors seem consciously to have avoided the most obvious words for 'leader' in their culture, presumably because they wanted to avoid buying in to the kinds of behaviour and organisation that were associated with that language.

35 In our time, too, the language of leadership was not minted in the church but (in significant part) borrowed from elsewhere. The explosion of the field of leadership training and leadership studies is often traced to the work of John Adair, who drew on his military and business experience to write *Training for Leadership* in 1968, before going on to become the world's first professor of leadership studies in 1979, at the University of Surrey.

36 There is little doubt that the church, in adopting the language of leadership, initially drew it at least in part from this and similar sources, and that it has gone on drawing from such sources as the secular leadership boom has advanced.[11] And it is not only the word 'leader' that has been borrowed but a whole vocabulary for describing the leader's task and goals. We speak of targets, key performance indicators, behavioural competencies, competition, entrepreneurship, risk management, effectiveness, growth and success. We can sound all but indistinguishable from our secular counterparts, at least from a distance, even to the point, at times, of echoing the high-octane glitz that accompanies some secular visions of the powerful leader.

---

11 There has also been a borrowing in the other direction: numerous authors working in the field of leadership studies have drawn on models from the Bible and the history of the church. See, for example, John Adair, *The Leadership of Jesus and its Legacy Today*, Norwich: Canterbury Press, 2011; Richard S. Ascough and Sandy Cotton, *Passionate Visionary: Leadership Lessons from the Apostle Paul*, Peabody, MA: Hendrickson, 2006; David Baron, *Moses on Management: 50 Leadership Lessons from the Greatest Manager of All Time*, New York, NY: Pocket Books, 1999; and many more.

37 Of course, the presence of language borrowed from secular sources is not itself proof that anything has gone wrong. Similarly, the fact that the language itself is a new borrowing does not mean that the practices and relationships that the language is now used to describe were previously absent from the church. New language can name existing realities, and do so tellingly. Nevertheless, the fact of this borrowing does pose, with considerable urgency, questions about what ways of thinking the church might inadvertently have borrowed when it took on this vocabulary, and whether in doing so it has bought into inappropriate patterns of behaviour, relationship and organisation. Has the appropriation of leadership language from secular sources been sufficiently critical?

2.3.2 The structures of leadership

38 The very existence of leadership studies as a distinct field with its own internal dynamics has suggested one way in which this question of critical appropriation can be pushed further.

39 In order to frame the question more clearly, it is helpful to begin with an initial, low-key definition of leadership. We might say that a leader is someone who assists others in the performance of a collective practice. Such a leader is not necessarily one who himself or herself excels in the practice, though he or she certainly has to be competent in it. Rather, he or she will be good at participating in that practice in such a way as to draw others deeper into it. Such a leader needs to be fully involved in the practice alongside others, but he or she also takes on some additional activities for the sake of this specific leadership role.

40 A healthy account of leadership will focus first and most insistently on the nature of the collective practice concerned. In relation to the church, therefore, our starting point is the whole people of God as they are called to serve God's mission in and for the world. The distinctive role of the leader can only be understood within and in relation to this calling of the whole people of God. The specific activities of leadership, together with the more generic processes of management, exist to assist, enable and inspire the people of God in their pursuit of this calling, and we should therefore take care that they are compatible with the church's purpose and genuinely feed it. The processes that build a healthy organisation (like finance and Human Resources) are absolutely vital to maintain the conditions that can allow the whole collective practice to function in the service of God's mission, and their absence can seriously damage the church's mission and ministry – but they are not ends in themselves. They are there, like leadership as a whole, only for the sake of the ministry and mission of the church.

41 We need to ask, however, whether the rise and rise of leadership as a dominant idea in the life of the church has led to a failure of this ordering of our attention. As we draw deeply on accounts of leadership developed with no connection to the church's ministry and mission, have we ended up *starting* with the specific activities of the leader, or with the specific demands of efficient management, and rearranging our understanding of ministry and mission around them?

2.3.3 The tasks of leadership

42 We need to ask, then, whether the church's increasing valorisation of leadership, because it has involved the adoption of generic accounts of leadership from secular sources, has led to a downplaying of the specific nature of the church, its ministry and mission. As well as asking whether this has involved turning away from the specific structure of ministry within which senior church leadership sits, we should ask whether it has involved turning away from the specific tasks that have been central to that ministry.

43 The descriptions of episcopal ministry in Canon C 18 and in the Common Worship Ordinal can provide a framework for asking this question. They do not describe a distinct activity of leadership, but rather distribute across several different headings the ways in which bishops will exercise what we might call leadership.[12] Bishops will

- be 'an example of righteous and godly living' (C 18), fashioning their lives 'according to the way of Christ' and leading the people 'in the way of holiness' (Ordinal);
- be the 'chief pastors' of the diocese, 'knowing their people and being known by them' (Ordinal), and being responsible for preserving and deepening the relationships of care that hold the church's life together;
- be teachers, whose task it is to 'uphold sound and wholesome doctrine, and to banish and drive away all erroneous and strange opinions' (C 18) so as to 'hand on entire' the Christian faith (Ordinal) – to ensure, including by example, the vitality of proclamation and the richness of teaching and formation;
- be 'the principal ministers' of the sacraments, called to 'lead the offering of prayer and praise' (Ordinal), and responsible for maintaining and developing the life of worship in the diocese, so that the focus of that life remains on God;
- discern and foster the gifts of the Spirit in all who follow Christ, commissioning them to minister in his name (Ordinal) and presiding over ordinations;
- be the people with responsibility for discipline, including the responsibility where necessary to 'correct and punish' (C18); and
- 'proclaim the gospel boldly, confront injustice and work for righteousness and peace in all the world' (Ordinal).

---

12 See http://www.churchofengland.org/about-us/structure/churchlawlegis/canons/section-c.aspx#Head1-78 and http://www.churchofengland.org/prayer-worship/worship/texts/ordinal/bishops.aspx.

44 Should we, therefore, think of leadership as a particular way of framing the tasks already on this list, or as an additional item to be appended to it, or both? And if it is an additional item, do we need to ask whether it proves, in practice, more important than some (or even all) of the other items on the list, and ends up vying with them for the limited time and energy that any one person has available? Is the idea of leadership the cuckoo in this nest?

2.3.4 The ethos of leadership

45 Some of the deepest questions about the increased focus on leadership in the life of the church have to do with the ethos of leadership. Has the focus on leadership led to a valorisation of attitudes and forms of behaviour and relationship that are not well suited to the church – that is, to the work of ministry and mission to which we are all called?

46 Do the virtues being demanded of senior leaders today sit uneasily with the virtues of discipleship? A Christian leader is, after all, a disciple first and a leader second, and that means that he or she is and remains a *follower* even while being a leader. Furthermore, as a disciple a leader is called to display the fruit of the Spirit – but some current models of leadership do not seem to place much emphasis on patience, kindness, gentleness and self-control, and might not sit easily with Canon C 18's description of the bishop's 'duty to set forward and maintain quietness, love, and peace among all'. How well do our descriptions of leadership cohere with our traditions of thinking (and arguing) about discipleship and holiness?

47 Do the relationships that leaders are currently being called to pursue conflict with the more basic patterns of relationship that the church is called to embody: patterns of gracious gift and reception among all God's people? 'Leader' is a relational term, but it is not always clear that the relationship envisaged between the leader and the led is the kind of relationship between members of the same body that Paul envisages in 1 Corinthians 12 and 13. How well do our descriptions of leadership cohere with our traditions of thinking (and arguing) about the nature of relationships in the body of Christ?

48 Do the expectations currently surrounding leaders focus on effectiveness and success in ways that undermine a distinctive Christian understanding of action, in which one's action is a gift that one receives more than it is something that one achieves; in which there can be no effectiveness without grace; and in which failure is one source of God's blessing? How well do our descriptions of leadership cohere with our traditions of thinking (and arguing) about the relationship between divine and human agency?

49 It is always worth asking whether our descriptions of leadership can leave room for a leader who was abandoned by all his followers, who was stripped of all dignity and power, and whose ministry was in every measurable sense defeated – and where that failure was nevertheless the foundation stone of God's mission. If Christ is our primary model of leadership, what does that do to our perception of the role? How well do our descriptions of leadership cohere with our traditions of thinking (and arguing) about the nature of Christ-like action?

2.4 For and against?

50 We have been speaking as if there were a straightforward opposition between the desire for stronger leadership and criticisms of the increased focus on leadership in the church. That does not, however, do justice to the situation in which we find ourselves. On both sides the same question is being asked: What is needed for the ministry and mission of the church to flourish?

51 That does not mean that there are no real differences between those who urge more focus on leadership and those who resist it, nor does it mean that the differences are trivial. It does mean, however, that these are differences that have arisen within a shared task – and it means that a response to both tendencies, the enthusiastic and the critical, requires the same thing: deeper attention to the nature of the church and its calling, and to the God who calls it. That is why it makes sense, at this point, to turn away from contemporary models for and claims about leadership, and to turn back to the New Testament.

3. Leadership in the New Testament[13]

52 Scripture holds a prime place as the source and guide for our 'faithful improvisation' (see §13 above). It teaches us to see the reality to which any account of Christian leadership must respond: the reality of God's call to the church. Attention to the New Testament church can provide a framework for faithful improvisation as we seek patterns of organisation, inspiration and fruitfulness for the twenty-first-century church.

53 We must, of course, beware the hermeneutical trap of thinking we just have to rediscover the primitive truth of some notional 'biblical pattern' and think ourselves back into it. In fact, one of the first conclusions we can draw from the study of the New Testament is that church order is never static: it keeps evolving to fit the ever-changing needs and challenges of a changing world. Arguably this is one of the prime tasks of 're-imagining ministry': the task of listening with attentiveness and sensitivity to the needs of God's world and the call of God's Spirit. But that listening process must also be attuned to the roots of our tradition, and to the words of Scripture: we need to look to the Bible, not for a transferable, once-for-all blueprint of church order, but for the fundamental principles ('canons') by which we can order the life of the church in our generation, responding to our world.

---

13 Section 3 of the report draws extensively on Loveday Alexander's 2011 Manson Memorial Lecture (Manchester, 20th October 2011) 'Paul the Apostle: Patterns of Ministry in the Pauline Churches'. Available online at bnts.org.uk under 'Seminar Groups/2013 Early Christianity'.

3.1 A triangular model of leadership

54 Theologies of church leadership tend to operate in one of two directions. A theology that starts with 'every-member ministry', with the mission and ministry of the whole people of God, can find itself struggling to provide a rationale for the particular calling of ordained ministry.[14] Conversely, a theology that starts with the ordained ministry can find itself caught in a defensive stance of making constant apologetic allusions to the mission and ministry of the whole people of God, without ever quite taking them seriously. Arguably, both models seriously distort the biblical pattern.

55 Rather than start with the church or its leaders, the pattern we propose starts with the action of God. It is God who calls and redeems a people to become a kingdom of priests and a holy nation (Exodus 19.6), and a light to the nations (Isaiah 49.6) – but it is also God who calls individuals to leadership within his people, starting with Moses, who embodies the three strands that become differentiated over Israel's history into kingly, priestly and prophetic leadership. Similarly, Jesus, the new Moses, is sent to be the pioneer (*archegos*) and shepherd of all God's people, embodying all three modes of leadership – but he also selects and calls a smaller group of disciples, sends them out and gives them authority to act in his name as his witnesses and surrogates. And, again, the gifts of the Spirit are given to the whole church – but that gifting is expressed in individual charismata (including the gift of leadership) exercised within the body of Christ (1 Corinthians 12.27–30; Ephesians 4.11–12).

56 This divine agency is variously experienced through the long history of the people of God. Its fundamentally Trinitarian shape is already expressed in Paul's classic formulation in 1 Corinthians

---

14 This problem is endemic in discussions about lay ministry. It is discussed more fully in the Faith and Order Advisory Group paper *The Mission and Ministry of the Whole Church: Biblical, Theological and Contemporary Perspectives*, London: Church House, 2007, available online at https://www.churchofengland.org/media/1229854/gsmisc%20854.pdf.

12.4–6: 'There are varieties of gifts, but the same Spirit; there are varieties of service, but the same Lord; and there are varieties of working, but it is the same God who inspires them all in every one.' The leadership of Christ is the leadership of the Word become incarnate, the eternal Son, and therefore a leadership from and in and into the life of the triune God.

57 Thus any theology of leadership in the church must begin with God's call: the primary exercise of leadership in the church is God's. In the first place, this is the calling of the whole people, who are called not by human 'leaders' but by God. But equally (and unapologetically), any theology of leadership in the church must acknowledge that God does call individuals to exercise leadership in and for the people of God. In turn, the leadership exercised by members of Christ's body is always a participation in his leadership of the whole people. The three – God, people and leaders – are linked in an irreducibly three-cornered relationship.

58 At a very simple level, we can represent the triangular dynamic of these relationships in the form of an equilateral triangle enclosed in a circle. In this diagram, the two 'sides' of the triangle represent this double calling: God calls his people; and God calls individuals to lead his people. The base of the triangle represents the complex two-way relationship between people and leaders – a relationship created by God's double call.

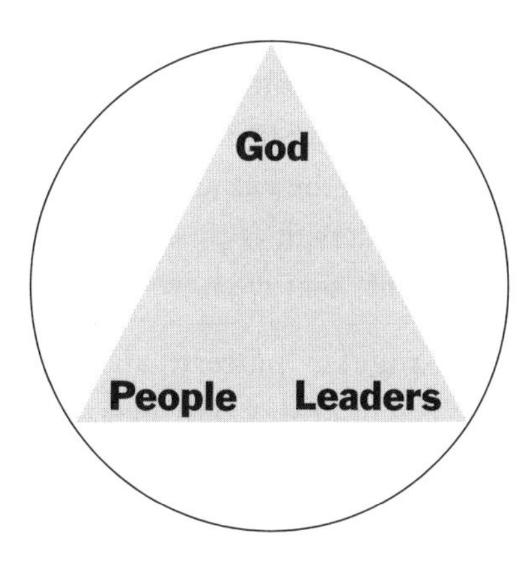

59 This first 'leadership triangle' offers a simple but fruitful template for analysing the grammar of ministry and leadership in the New Testament. It enables us to mine a rich vein of teaching material on leadership and ministry (especially, though not solely, in Paul's letters), and it brings out the essential relationship between God's calling of God's people and God's calling of leaders for that people. It makes it clear at the outset that the narrower concerns of 'leadership training' (focusing on relationships between leaders and people, or interactions between leaders) form only one aspect of a multifaceted relationship with the Lord of the church, who calls both the church and its leaders to his service.

60 A fuller description would also need to take account of the external relationships of the church. In the diagram, the circle represents the world, touching the triangle at three points. It is important to note that God's interactions with the world are not confined to the church; similarly, the meaningful interactions of Christians and their leaders with the world are not confined to their internal interactions with each other – though too often we speak and act as if they were.

61 Theologically speaking, of course, it is misleading to confine God to the apex of the triangle. This is a simplified diagram with a strictly limited theological remit. It does not attempt to represent every aspect of the life of God within the life of the church (how could it?). The people of God have the Spirit at work within them and Christ incarnate in their midst. They live in relation to the Father because they are being drawn by the Spirit to share in the Son's relationship to the Father. When we talk about God's calling of people and leaders, it is this triune action of God drawing us into God's own life that we have in mind.

62 A similar triangular pattern also offers a fruitful way of representing the interplay between the apostles and the leaders of local churches in the New Testament. The underlying three-cornered pattern remains constant: God calls and empowers both the church and its leaders, entrusting both with a *diakonia*, a commission to bring God's word and God's pastoral care to a world in need.[15] Right from the start, however, the New Testament presents us with a dual-focus picture of leadership, with one focus on the local congregations and the other on the apostolic networks that operate at trans-local level. This dual-location leadership pattern can be seen clearly across the later writings of the New Testament (see Hebrews 13.7, 17, 24; 1 Peter 5.1–5). It is also classically expressed in Paul's Miletus speech (Acts 20.17–35), where Paul, deeply conscious of his own calling as an apostle (20.24), reminds the Ephesian elders that their leadership, too, is derived from the Holy Spirit (20.28).

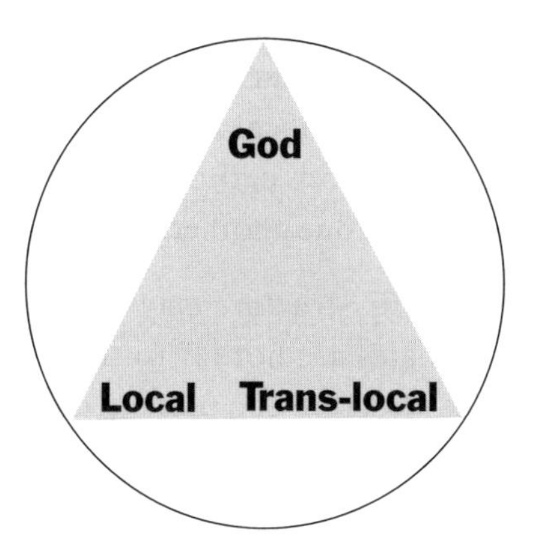

63 We therefore need a second, supplementary triangle in order to do justice to the increased geographical complexity of the growing church.[16] Just as, in the light of God's call, there is a necessary interplay between leaders and people, so there is a necessary interplay between local and trans-local leaders in the light of the same call. In each case, understanding how that

15 For this understanding of *diakonia*, see John N. Collins, *Diakonia: Re-interpreting the Ancient Sources*, New York: Oxford University Press, 1990.

16 Our two triangles are not the same. That is, the second triangle is not simply a re-labelling of the first. As we will be explaining, for example, leaders can be both local and trans-local. In a 3D model, the two triangles could be combined as two faces of a pyramid.

interplay works in relation to God's defining action is central to the task of understanding New Testament visions of leadership.

64 Historically speaking, this deep-seated duality may provide a more robust foundation for a theology of church leadership than mistaken attempts to read back the three-fold order of bishops, priests and deacons wholesale into the New Testament – or (equally mistaken) attempts to deny that the New Testament church has any order at all. But it may also provide an enduring thread for theological engagement with the shape of church leadership, a pattern that resurfaces time and again in church history, in new configurations but with the same underlying tension between local and global.[17] It is the creative interplay (and tension) between these two that ensures both the locality of the church and what we call its 'catholicity' – that is, the fact that its various local manifestations are together parts of one body, the church catholic, and are called to live in deep communion with one another.

65 Such a leadership structure may seem impossibly complex, but, in fact, analogies are not far to seek. We might, for example, compare the structure of a modern orchestra, where the 'leader' of the orchestra is neither the owner nor the employer of the orchestra but the (elected) leader of a collegial body of independent musicians. Another level of leadership (itinerant, trans-local, visionary, charismatic) is offered by the conductors who visit the orchestra and lead it in performance: their relationship is symbolised by the handshake between conductor and leader at the end of a performance. But both would claim to be operating in the service of a higher allegiance to the music itself, offering an interpretation, articulation or embodiment of the composer's designs. To quote the conductor Bernhard Haitink, 'It's not about power ... It's not about me imposing

17 Liberation theologians have done some helpful thinking on this: see, for example, Robert Schreiter, *Constructing Local Theologies*, Maryknoll, NY: Orbis 2008. See also *Fresh Expressions in the Mission of the Church: Report of an Anglican–Methodist Working Party*, London: Church House, 2012.

my wonderful interpretation on the music ... It's about motivating ... making space ... about practising musicianship with musicians.'[18]

3.2 The language of leadership in the New Testament

What terms are used for leadership roles in the New Testament?

What areas of secular life does the church mine for leadership models?

What analogies or metaphors are used to describe church leadership in the New Testament?

66 This 'triangular' structure is deeply embedded in the language used for church leadership in the New Testament. Its writers consistently avoid using words associated with political or military power to describe the church's human leaders. In the world of the New Testament, the word 'leader' (*hegemon*) is used only to refer to royal or imperial governors like Pilate (Matthew 27.2). If the church has a 'governor', it is the royal Messiah predicted by the prophet Micah (Matthew 2.6), the 'pioneer (*archegos*) and perfecter of our faith' (Hebrews 12.2). Only in three passages do we find the related term *hegoumenos* ('one who leads/guides') used of church leaders: in the Epistle to the Hebrews (Hebrews 13.7, 17, 24), in Acts (Acts 15.22) and in Luke's Gospel (Luke 22.26).

67 The last passage is crucial for understanding the ethos of leadership in the church. Here Jesus at the Last Supper is responding to the disciples' quarrel over who should be the greatest: 'The kings of the nations lord it over them, and those in authority over them are called benefactors. Not so with you;

18 Interviewed on BBC Radio 3, June 2014.

instead the one who is greatest among you must become like the youngest, and the one who leads (*ho hegoumenos*) like the one who serves (*ho diakonon*).' Note that Jesus does not forbid the use of the term 'leader': he accepts that there are (or will be) differences of role and status among his followers. But his words show an awareness of the political connotations of 'leadership' language, and he offers a radical redefinition of what 'leadership' must mean in the context of his own servant ministry and forthcoming death (v.27). Right at the outset, then, we are faced with the paradox of leadership in the New Testament. There is leadership in the New Testament church – plenty of it, as we shall see in the next section – but there is already a sensitivity about leadership language and about the status associations it brings with it.

68 The terms used for church leadership are very fluid in the New Testament, with an emphasis on function rather than title. Paul's famous list of ministries in 1 Corinthians 12.28 veers between recognised roles (apostle, prophet, teacher) and spiritual gifts (healing, miracles, tongues). Not all of these are leadership roles: the whole point of the body analogy is that the Spirit-gifted church exhibits a whole variety of 'ministries' (*diakoniai*, 12.5) working together for the good of the whole. In modern English translations, 'leadership' appears in the list as one gift among many: in the skills of the pilot (*kuberneseis*), often used by ancient writers as a metaphor for political leadership; or in the advocacy and support offered by the skilled administrator (*antilempseis*, 12.28). In the parallel list in Romans 12.6–8, 'leadership' sometimes appears as a translation of *ho proistamenos*, the one prepared to 'stand out' in the assembly and to 'stand up' for the rights of weaker members.

69 If political power-terms are generally avoided, what areas of contemporary life does the New Testament mine for leadership models? Language is never neutral: the terms used by the early church reflect the social models that formed the matrix of the church's formative years. Some of these are obvious. From the contemporary Jewish community comes the *presbyteros* ('elder' or 'senior'), and perhaps the *apostolos*, which may be a distant echo of the *shaliach* or 'delegate' used by the High Priest to keep in touch with scattered Jewish communities. The teacher and the disciple (or 'learner') come from the world of the schools. Some are less obvious. The *diakonos* (Romans 16.2) taps into the 'upstairs–downstairs' world of the household, the primary unit of business as well as of family life in the ancient world.[19] The *prostatis* (Romans 16.2) draws on the world of ancient patronage, a world where people with status and wealth were expected to use it on behalf of others.[20] And what of the *episkopos* (Philippians 1.1; 1 Timothy 3.1)? A number of different backgrounds have been suggested for this (perhaps deliberately) colourless term: the 'inspector' or 'overseer' on a large estate, the financial officer of a voluntary association, or even the *Mebaqqer* or spiritual overseer of the Essene communities.[21]

70 A similar variety of social worlds is reflected in the analogies and metaphors used by New Testament writers to capture the ethos of leadership in the church. Paul describes himself in turn as father (1 Thessalonians 2.11), nurse (1 Thessalonians 2.7) and steward (1 Corinthians 4.1–5) to the churches he has founded – all household terms. The architect and the gardener (1 Corinthians 3.5–10) belong to the world of the great estates. Rather more unusual are the matchmaker or marriage broker

---

19 John N. Collins argues that 'the underlying notion of *diakonia* is that of a "go-between"', with the focus on 'fetching or bringing things on call' rather than on menial status. But the evidence he assembles demonstrates that the word is most commonly used of household attendants: see Collins, *Diakonia*, pp. 87–9. Cf. Loveday Alexander, '*Diakonia, the Ephesian Comma, and the Ministry of All Believers*', in Jason A. Whitlark et al. (eds), *Interpretation and the Claims of the Text: Resourcing New Testament Theology*, Waco, TX: Baylor University Press, 2014, pp. 159–76, at p. 164.

20 On the *prostatis*, see Wayne Meeks, *The First Urban Christians: The Social World of the Apostle Paul*, New Haven, CT: Yale University Press, 1983, pp. 74–110; and Caroline Whelan, 'Amica Pauli: The Role of Phoebe in the Early Church', *Journal for the Study of the New Testament* 49 (1993), pp. 67–85.

21 For a survey of recent scholarship on the *episkopos*, see Alistair C. Stewart, *The Original Bishops: Office and Order in the First Christian Communities*, Grand Rapids, MI: Baker Academic, 2014.

(2 Corinthians 11.2) and the ambassador, pleading on Christ's behalf (2 Corinthians 5.20) to effect a reconciliation between God and his wayward people. What is striking about many of these terms is the way in which they draw attention to an essential aspect of the self-understanding of Christian leaders in the New Testament. They are used to distance the authority of the leader from any sense of ownership or mastery, and to deflect attention back to the Lord of the church, who is the real source of the leader's authority. They reflect what we may call a refracted authority, seen through a triangular prism that resists the construction of top-down management structures.

71 Particularly important in the emergent vocabulary of Christian leadership are two metaphors which already have a long Old Testament pedigree. When Paul describes himself and Apollos as 'stewards of the mysteries of God' (1 Corinthians 4.1), he is stressing that he is not the master of the household (the employer, in modern terms) but a fellow-employee, tasked with supplying his fellow-servants with all they need to carry out the master's orders. This imagery (echoed in many of the Gospel parables – see especially Luke 12.41–48) carries with it a strong sense of accountability. The idea that the steward will ultimately have to 'give account' when the master returns is linked with a strongly eschatological view of the church (see Hebrews 13.17; Luke 16.1–13; Matthew 25.14–30). Behind it lies a long association of leadership with stewardship (see, for example, Isaiah 22.15–25).

72 A similar pattern of relationships underpins the familiar image of the leader as 'shepherd' or 'pastor' (Ephesians 4.11). The Gospel image of Jesus as the Good Shepherd who seeks out the lost and leads his sheep in and out to find pasture (John 10; see also Luke 15.3–7; Matthew 18.10–14) echoes the Old Testament language of God as the shepherd of his people (e.g. Psalms 77.20, 78.52–73, 80.1, 100.3), and especially Ezekiel's prophecy that God himself will shepherd his people, pasture them and bind up their wounds (Ezekiel 34). In John 21.15–17, Jesus invites Peter to be his under-shepherd ('Feed my sheep!') – a role which will eventually be shared with other, local leaders (1 Peter 5.2–4; cf. Acts 20.28). The image of the shepherd has been richly mined in Christian reflection on leadership, offering a pastoral model of leadership that is at once active and bold (David in 1 Samuel 17.34–35), tender and caring (Psalm 23; Ezekiel 34.4) and ultimately sacrificial (John 10.11). In Christian thought, the image of the shepherd is never very far from that of the servant who offers himself 'as a lamb to the slaughter' (Isaiah 53.7; cf. John 1.36; Revelation 5.6).[22]

3.3 The structures of leadership in the New Testament

73 The church has always adapted its structures in response to changing needs, and the New Testament reflects the still fluid structures of the church's first decades. It gives us a dual-location leadership structure of local and trans-local leaders, working in partnership and each owing allegiance to the Lord who calls and empowers both. This is represented diagrammatically in our second triangle above. Neither of these is more 'essential' than the other.[23] Both are equally exercised within the body of Christ and derive their validity from the only 'essential' leadership within the church, which is that of Christ himself.[24]

---

22 Paul Minear, *Images of the Church in the New Testament,* Cambridge: James Clarke, 2007), pp. 84–9.

23 Kenneth E. Kirk (ed.), *The Apostolic Ministry: Essays on the History and Doctrine of Episcopacy,* London: Hodder & Stoughton, 1946, pp. 7–14.

24 As T.W. Manson observed many years ago. See *The Church's Ministry*, London: Hodder & Stoughton, 1953, p. 30.

3.3.1 Leadership in the local church

74 We begin with Paul's letters, which provide our earliest first-hand records of the inner life of the early church. In order to understand how Paul's theology of leadership works, we need to begin with his ecclesiology, his theological vision of the church as the people of God. Fundamental to this ecclesiology is a three-way relationship between the apostle, the *ekklesia* (which for Paul mostly means the local church) and the God who calls and empowers both. This triangular set of relationships is deeply embedded in the grammar of the letters. Each local *ekklesia* is a local instantiation of the people of God, called into being by God and sanctified by his grace. Paul's letters are grounded in the confidence that the whole ekklesia is the recipient of the gifts of the Spirit; the whole *ekklesia* is called to be God's holy people, the visible sign of the presence of God in a particular locality (1 Corinthians 1.2–9).

75 But right from the start there are signs of a progressive differentiation of functions and ministries: 'There are varieties of gifts (*charismata*), but the same Spirit; there are varieties of ministries (*diakoniai*), but the same Lord; there are varieties of working (*energemata*), but it is the same God whose energy [literally 'in-working'] produces them all in every one' (1 Corinthians 12.4–6, our translation). As the body of Christ, the church embodies the active presence of Christ in the world, doing the things that Jesus did: teaching, healing, preaching the kingdom of God. But these activities are now distributed among many 'members', rather than being concentrated in one person (1 Corinthians 12; Romans 12.3–8).

76 These varied ministries (*diakoniai*) are not the preserve of an ordained ministry or a leadership elite but are the responsibility of the whole church. The lists of *charismata* are dominated by the **ministry of the word**: wisdom and knowledge, teaching and instruction, encouragement and exhortation, prophecy and revelation, the gift of tongues and their interpretation. Alongside this is the **practical, pastoral work** of the church: healing and miracles, financial aid and almsgiving, advocacy and social support. The **worship** of the church is enriched by contributions from all its members, whether in words of prophecy and exhortation, in psalms and hymns (1 Corinthians 14; Colossians 3), or in sharing the bread and wine of the Eucharist (1 Corinthians 10, 11).

77 Where does 'leadership' fit into this dynamic picture of the local church? Paul's letters provide clear evidence that certain people within the congregation perform a range of functions that we would associate with 'leadership' (1 Thessalonians 5.12–13; 1 Corinthians 16.15–18; Philippians 4.2–4; Romans 16). Many of these local leaders, it is fair to assume, were the hosts of house-churches. This is where we find the church's first *episkopoi* and *diakonoi* (Philippians 1.1; Romans 16.2). This leadership is fluid and flexible, part of the gifting and energising activity of God in the local church. Here we see the pattern represented by our first leadership triangle above. God's call and gifting are the source from which flow the whole ministry and mission of the church; within that ministry and mission, God calls some to specific ministries of leadership.

78 The book of Acts gives us a more comprehensive picture of local church leadership. Acts 6 sees a division of labour between the apostles and the local officers selected by the congregation to 'serve tables', that is, to oversee the church's charitable activities – though two of those appointed, Stephen and Philip, prove to have a wider role in mission (Acts 7, 8). The church in Antioch has its own leadership of 'prophets and teachers'; it is they who appoint Saul and Barnabas as *apostoloi* or delegates of the church, sent out on mission (13.1–3) and reporting back to the church on their return (14.26–28). The churches of Lycaonia and Ephesus have 'elders' (*presbuteroi*), the former at least appointed by Paul (14.23, 20.17). So does the church in Jerusalem, sitting under the presidency of James – though how these elders were appointed, and who gave them their authority, is never stated.

79 Thus, the first 'order of ministry' in the church of the New Testament is the *laos*, the people of God, living out their calling to be God's people in the particular locality where they live. This 'locality', localisation in a particular place, is part of the essence of what it means to be the church, something essential to its well-being. Within these local churches there is a proliferation of multiple forms of local ministry, the concrete evidence and outworking of the divine energy: *because* God is at work in you, there are varieties of gifts and varieties of ministries (1 Corinthians 12.4–6). And among those gifts is the gift of leadership. The church needs a leadership that is rooted in, listening to and answerable to a particular *local* community.[25]

3.3.2 Trans-local leadership: apostles

80 However, leadership in the New Testament is not limited to the local church. Right from the start, Paul's letters testify to the exercise of spiritual leadership over distance and over time, maintaining and building up contacts over time and space. This *trans-local* dimension is reinforced through the greetings at the end of each epistle, as well as through practical projects like the collection for the poor among the saints in Jerusalem, which absorbed so much of Paul's energies in the latter years of his mission (2 Corinthians 8–9).

81 Paul is not alone in exercising this trans-local apostolic calling. Other travelling apostles, including Peter (Cephas) exercised a right to hospitality and subsistence at the expense of the local church (1 Corinthians 9.5). The travelling apostles are not delegates *of* other local churches, or even of the Jerusalem church (Galatians 1–2): their authority is in some way behind and above that of the network of local churches. Nor is their authority tied to particular regions, like the bishops of later centuries. Paul has a clear view of his own calling to the Gentiles (Galatians

---

25 Cf. Croft, *Ministry in Three Dimensions*, pp. 70–2.

2.1–10) and of his own segment of the map (Romans 15.19). But this demarcation does not prevent Peter from visiting Corinth, or Paul from planning to visit Rome (Romans 15.22–24). Their apostolic oversight is exercised across the whole church of God. And it is derived not from a church (not even the church of Jerusalem) but from Christ himself.

82 The Gospels and Acts provide the narrative basis for this apostolic calling. The narrative of Acts is dominated by the risen Christ, instructing 'the apostles whom he had chosen', eating with them and commissioning them: 'You shall be my witnesses ... to the ends of the earth' (Acts 1.1–8). With the dispersal of the growing church (Acts 8.1ff), the apostles assume a more itinerant *episkope*, leaving it to James and the elders to look after the affairs of the Jerusalem church. Acts also testifies to other forms of trans-local ministry: Agabus the prophet, Philip the evangelist and Apollos the wisdom teacher (Acts 11, 8, 19). But these charismatic offices (like the 'apostles and prophets' of the *Didache*) offer itinerant ministry rather than itinerant *leadership:* they have their own spiritual gifts but they do not have the trans-local authority that marks the *episkope* of the apostles.

83 Thus, there is no place in biblical ecclesiology for the go-it-alone church: catholicity, connectedness, is built in to the church's DNA right from the start. This connectedness may be expressed in different ways in different traditions: 'But that it should happen cannot be open to discussion, for in it a dimension of the church is expressed which belongs to its essence: its catholicity, that is to say its unity in the truth through space and time. This dimension of catholicity is given with the Gospel itself and therefore with the ministry of proclamation in preaching and sacrament in itself.'[26]

---

26 Dorothea Wendebourg, 'The Reformation in Germany and the Episcopal Office', in Ingolf Dalferth and Ruper Hoare (eds), *Visible Unity and the Ministry of Oversight: The Second Theological Conference Held under the Meissen Agreement between the Church of England and the Evangelical Church in Germany*, London: Church House Publishing, 1997, pp. 49–78, at p. 54.

3.4 The tasks of leadership in the New Testament

What do New Testament church leaders do? What tasks are they expected to perform? How is the role of leader conceptualised, and how does it change and develop over time?

3.4.1 Leadership and ministry

84 Leadership is first and foremost a form of ministry (*diakonia*: 1 Corinthians 16.15). It is one of the multifarious forms of 'ministry' that mark the Spirit's continuing gift to the church (1 Corinthians 12.4–6; Ephesians 4.11). All leaders are ministers, but not all ministers are leaders. Leadership is a gift of the Spirit, but not all those with spiritual gifts are leaders. Thus, in Paul's vision of the spiritually gifted church, 'leadership' is one ministry among many. As Matthew Henry puts it: 'our Lord Jesus Christ, when he ascended on high, left something for all his servants to do ... All are appointed to work, and some authorised to rule.'[27]

85 Many of the tasks that we now associate with church leaders (worship, word and work) were, in the Pauline churches, regarded as the responsibility of the whole church. With the passing of time, more of these ministries came to be concentrated in the persons of the local leaders. It is important to keep in mind the distinction between the specific task of 'leadership' and the varied ministry tasks that church leaders have accumulated over time.

86 This distinction can be helpfully formulated in terms of *episkope* ('oversight'). For Paul, teaching and exhortation, healing and tongues, practical aid and pastoral care are all gifts of the Spirit

---

27 Matthew Henry, *Commentary on the Whole Bible*, London, 1721, on Mark 13.28–37; available online at http://www.ccel.org/ccel/henry/mhc5.Mark.xiv.html.

to the whole people of God. When the sacred assembly (*ekklesia*) is convened, any one of the congregation may lead in worship (1 Corinthians 11.4–5; 14.5, 26). But there is a downside to this charismatic fecundity. Paul's comments in 1 Corinthians 14 show the apostle's concern for what is missing: the need for clarity of message (vv.6–12); the need to make the church a space where outsiders can recognise the presence of God (vv.20–25); and, crucially, the need for 'building up' the *whole* church (vv.1–5; 27–33). His critique is not of the charismatic freedom of Corinthian worship but of its self-centredness: prayer, praise and prophecy are not matters for spiritual self-indulgence but need to be directed to support the life of the whole church.

87 We can see here in embryo one of the basic criteria for leadership: leaders respond to God's call not merely to fulfil their own ministry but to build up the ministries of others. Leadership lies precisely in that wider vision, that looking out for the needs of the whole church – what later generations would call 'oversight' (*episkope*). Leadership has a vision for clarity of message, openness to the world, and the building up of the whole church. Leaders (in other words) are distinguished not so much for performing distinct tasks as for ordering and building up the ministries of the whole congregation on behalf of and in the interests of all, both inside and outside the church. Thus, the fundamental task of leadership is to 'preside', to take charge, to become 'the one who stands in front' (*ho proistamenos*: Romans 12.8; 1 Thessalonians 5.12).[28] Leadership is prepared to take responsibility, to take the risk of 'standing out' from the crowd, but knows that this can only be done 'in the Lord'.

---

28 In Justin (c. 150 CE) the same verb is used of the one who 'presides' at the Eucharist, in *First Apology* 65.3–5. See Denis Minns and Paul Parvis (eds), *Justin, Philosopher and Martyr: Apologies*, Oxford: Oxford University Press, 2009.

3.4.2 The tasks of local leadership

88 We can already see in this early period a process of change and development in the way that different ministries are distributed between the people of God (the *laos*), the local *episkopoi* and the trans-local leadership of the apostles. For convenience, we can divide these tasks into four areas: **word, worship, work** and the wider **world.**

89 **Word:** Ministries of the word played a large part in the worship of the Pauline congregations: prophecy and teaching, tongues and revelations. Within this wider ministry, leaders are specially entrusted with a ministry of exhortation (*paraklesis*), for the building up of the body of Christ, and admonition or moral discipline (*nouthesia*). Their task is to take responsibility for the moral and spiritual welfare of the whole body – 'to lose sleep over your souls', as Hebrews 13.17 puts it. Paul sums up this hortatory and disciplinary aspect of leadership in 1 Thessalonians 5.14: 'Admonish the unruly, comfort the discouraged, help the weak, be patient with all.' Admonition must always be combined with encouragement – and with self-awareness (Galatians 6.1; Acts 20.28).

90 **Worship:** Leadership is concerned with **order** (1 Corinthians 14.40), whether in the ordering of charismatic worship so that all may participate and all may be edified, or in the arrangements for sharing the Lord's Supper so that none goes hungry (1 Corinthians 11.27–34). It is precisely this commitment to **fellowship** or 'sharing' (*koinonia*), this concern to put your brother's or sister's interests before your own, that lies at the heart of the Lord's Supper: which is why the eucharistic pattern of self-giving love is central to the life of the church (1 Corinthians 11.23–26, 10.14–22). Given that many of these local leaders were the hosts of house-churches, it is not surprising that **hospitality** is an essential aspect of their role (Romans 16; see also Philemon 1; Acts 16; Romans 12.13; Hebrews 13.2; 1 Timothy 3.2; Titus 1.8; 1 Peter 4.9; 3 John). It seems likely, if only for practical reasons, that such hosts would have 'presided' at the common meal: eucharistic presidency (and baptism) was at this early stage an aspect of local (not apostolic) leadership.[29]

91 **Work:** Leadership involves labouring for the welfare of the people. Each member of the body is called to work for the good of the others (1 Corinthians 10.24) – but leaders are called to the distinctive task of keeping this good work circulating. The term *prostates/prostatis* (Romans 16.2) has the sense 'patron, benefactor, champion'. Those in positions of honour and distinction were expected to act on behalf of others, to offer advocacy and leadership to the vibrant and active programmes of almsgiving and pastoral care that characterised the life of the early churches. Such active and practical leadership is hard work (*kopos*).[30] It demands all the commitment that a mature adult would give to the daily task of earning a living.

92 **The wider world:** The task of 'presidency' (*prostasia*) also has a representative aspect: those who preside also represent their community to the outside world. Local leaders act as *de facto* connection points with the trans-local leadership of the apostles. It is the local leaders who receive Paul's letters and who are solemnly charged with making them known to the congregation (1 Thessalonians 5.27). They take letters and gifts to Paul (1 Corinthians 16.17–18; Philippians 2.25–30) and carry letters from Paul to other churches (Romans 16.1–2).

3.4.3 The tasks of apostolic leadership

93 The fundamental apostolic task is summed up in Jesus' farewell mandate to his disciples: 'You shall be my witnesses' (Acts 1.8). To be an apostle is to be a delegate; apostles are 'sent' not by

---

29 For house-church hosts as prototypical local leaders, see Harry O. Maier, *The Social Setting of the Ministry as Reflected in the Writings of Hermas, Clement and Ignatius*, Waterloo, Ontario: Wilfrid Laurier University Press, 1991.

30 1 Thessalonians 5.12; see also 1 Corinthians 16.16; Romans 16.6, 12.

the church but by Christ himself to be his witnesses 'to the ends of the earth'. The apostolic task thus has a global (or trans-local) dimension built into it from the outset. The components of this global task are spelt out in more detail in Matthew 28.19–20: mobility, making disciples, baptising and teaching.

94 **Word:** The task of making the gospel known in the wider world is essential to the apostolic task. The apostles are called to make disciples: that is, to take on Jesus' task of **preaching** the kingdom and calling people to follow him (Mark 1.17; Acts 20.24–25; Romans 1.5). Paul conceives his task primarily in terms of mission and outreach, planting the seed (1 Corinthians 3.6) and opening up new areas to the gospel (Romans 15.20). Equally important is the task of **teaching**, instructing new disciples in the essentials of the faith (Acts 2.42) and strengthening and encouraging their growth through exhortation and admonition. Paul combines church planting and outreach with a ministry of 'building up' through letters and repeated visits (Acts 14.22; 20.1, 31). The Jerusalem apostles have a particular responsibility for preserving and passing on the stories of Jesus and the Scripture passages that unlock their meaning (Luke 24.44–49) – a tradition that Paul passes on to his congregations (1 Corinthians 11.23–26, 15.3–8). The apostolic witness is about keeping the scattered congregations in touch with their common roots in Christ, not only in words but also by providing a **model** of the Christ-shaped life (1 Corinthians 4.15–16, 11.1; Philippians 3.17).

95 **Worship**: Equally fundamental to the whole apostolic task is **prayer** (see Acts 6.4). This is expressed graphically in Paul's letters, where the opening prayer places all their mutual relationships within a 'triangular' framework: this is not just about me and you, but about you, me and God. The apostolic task also involves challenging their hearers to enter the sacramental life of the church (Matthew. 28.20). In Acts, apostolic preaching is integrally connected with repentance, faith and baptism (Acts 2, 16), with receiving the gift of the

Spirit (Acts 8, 19) and with entering a eucharistic community (Acts 2.42). As the church grows and spreads, apostolic leadership is exercised not in a monopoly of sacramental ministry but in oversight (*episkope*) for the proper ordering of the sacraments and in the passing on of dominical tradition (1 Corinthians 10–11, 15).

96 Work: In a very direct way, the apostles in Acts are depicted as carrying on the work of Christ in healing and pastoral care (Acts 3.6; 9.34, 40; 20.10; 28.8). But the work of caring for the poor is the task of the whole church (Acts 4.34–35), and Acts depicts a progressive division of labour as the apostles effectively entrust the tasks of administrative and pastoral *diakonia* to the local church (Acts 6.1–6, 11.30). This frees them up for a wider *episkope*, initially in Samaria and Judaea (Acts 9–10), later as far afield as Corinth (1 Corinthians 1.12, 9.5). For Paul, the 'work' (*kopos*) of leadership is shared with his co-workers (*sunergoi*) in local leadership (Romans 16). However, he speaks more than once of the physical and mental hardships peculiar to the apostolic task (1 Corinthians 4.9–13; 2 Corinthians 11.16–33), not least what he calls 'the care of all the churches' (2 Corinthians 11.28). This trans-local *episkope* entails a significant commitment of time and administrative skill, not only in travel but in the deployment of his own staff team, in correspondence with individual churches and in the organisation of the collection for the poor in Jerusalem (2 Corinthians 8–9).[31] Work, in the sense of earning a living, is also a part of the apostolic lifestyle: Paul's commitment to self-supporting ministry, freeing up surplus funds for charitable work, serves as a pattern for local leaders (Acts 20.33–35; 2 Thessalonians 3.7–9).

---

31 On the collection, see 1 Corinthians 16.1–4; 2 Corinthians 8–9; Romans 15.25–33. For a full recent discussion, see Bruce Longenecker, *Remember the Poor: Paul, Poverty, and the Greco-Roman World*, Grand Rapids, MI: William B. Eerdmans, 2010.

97 **The wider world**: The apostolic task is global: its boundaries are 'the ends of the earth' (an astonishingly bold vision for this tiny group at the edge of the Roman empire). This global horizon has two components. The first is **networking** between scattered churches. Paul's commitment to catholicity entails a significant expenditure of energy, keeping the networks alive by a variety of means, including letters, visits and greetings (see, for example, Romans 16; 1 Corinthians 1.2, 4.17). Secondly, the apostles represent the public face of the church not only in evangelism but in **apologetic**. The interface with the wider world is essential to the apostolic task (both for Paul and the Twelve) – and they encounter in their persons both its incomprehension and its hostility (Luke 21.12–19; Acts 9.15–16). The apostolic call to witness (*marturia*) may also be a call to martyrdom (John 21.19). Apologetic speech – speech to those outside the church – occupies a significant amount of dramatic space in Acts, and Paul alludes to this role (and to its impact on the confidence of the church) in the epistles (Philippians 1.12–18).

3.5 Becoming a leader in the New Testament

98 How are leaders selected and authorised in the New Testament? Who appoints them? On what basis are they chosen? What is the role of vocation, selection and discernment in this process? Is it acceptable to put yourself forward for a leadership role? Here, again, the subtle interplay of divine and human agency represented by our 'triangular' pattern comes to the fore on the (rare) occasions when the New Testament lifts the lid on the forms of selection and discernment that lie behind the process of becoming a leader.

99 Leadership is not *sought* but *given*. It is a commission, a trust, a command. The initiative in calling and equipping leaders comes from God. Moses and the prophets hear the call of God.

David is picked out, the youngest and most improbable of a line of brothers, by the prophet Samuel in response to the active prompting of the divine voice. Time and again, biblical leaders greet this sense of divine calling with surprise, reluctance, suspicion, unbelief.

100 The paradigm of divine calling is clearly set out in the Gospels. Jesus calls his disciples from their daily occupations (fishing, tax-collecting) to 'leave everything and follow me'. He chooses the Twelve for the more specific task of becoming apostles, gives them authority and sends them out to act as his agents in the mission of the kingdom. He promises that they will be empowered by the Holy Spirit – a promise that is fulfilled after the resurrection (John 20; Acts 1–2).

101 In Acts 1.15–26, the believers cast lots to discover the one whom God has chosen to take Judas' place in the college of apostles. After Pentecost, however, the gift of the Spirit becomes the determining factor in the selection and commissioning of leaders. But this is not a magical process: the Spirit's work graciously includes human agency by freeing and eliciting a faithful response. Thus, in Acts 6, faced with a manifest practical need for assistance with the distribution of charity, the apostles ask the assembled body of believers to choose suitable candidates 'filled with the Spirit'. The apostles' laying on of hands, *with prayer*, is both a commissioning and a way of invoking the divine agency over this new ministry. Similarly, Paul hears the voice of God in vision and dream, but it needs the obedience of Ananias and the discernment of Barnabas to help him fully realise his apostolic calling (Acts 9, 11), culminating in the laying on of hands, *with prayer and fasting*, by the prophets and teachers of Antioch (Acts 13.1–3) – both an act of commissioning and an act of entrusting the work (and the workers) to God (cf. Acts 14.23, 26).

102 This intermeshing of divine and human agency is replicated in the appointment of local leaders in the Pauline churches. Paul himself says of Stephanas and his colleagues in Corinth that they 'appointed themselves to the ministry' (1 Corinthians 16.15). Nevertheless, he makes every effort to endorse and support their leadership, both by personal commendation and visits, and more generally by including them in his army of 'co-workers' (Romans 16). These local ministries are also seen as out-workings of the divine energy – gifts of the Spirit exercised within the body of Christ. This divine origin precludes boasting (Romans 12.3; 1 Corinthians 1.31, 3.21; 2 Corinthians 4.6ff) and competitiveness (1 Corinthians 12–14). But it also confers real authority – an authority that demands respect (1 Thessalonians 5.12–13; 1 Corinthians 16.15).

103 In Acts 20, in a speech that is paradigmatic for New Testament leadership, Paul instructs a group of elders: 'Take heed to yourselves and to the whole flock in which the Holy Spirit has made you overseers (*episkopoi*), to shepherd the church of God, which he purchased through his own blood' (Acts 20.28). However it is mediated, leadership (*episkope*) is a gift of the Holy Spirit to the whole church, held in trust under the Chief Shepherd to whom the flock ultimately belongs (see 1 Peter 5.1–5; John 21).

104 This pervasive sense of divine calling results in a very real sense of compulsion – or obedience. The prophet cannot resist the call of God. Isaiah's 'Woe is me!' is echoed in Paul's 'Woe is me if I preach not the Gospel!' (Isaiah 6; 1 Corinthians 9). Whatever their natural feelings of unworthiness or hesitation, those called to leadership cannot refuse. As Paul says in a different context, the gifts and the calling of God are irrevocable (Romans 11) and much will be required of those to whom much is given (Matthew 25.14–30). The charism of leadership, like other gifts of the Spirit, is not a personal gift to the individual, a matter for personal career development, but a gift to the church (Ephesians 4.7–12; Hebrews 2.4), a gift held in trust, to be used in the service of the Giver.

105 Those who have gifts (and that may include quite practical gifts honed in the secular world – see Romans 12.6–8; 1 Corinthians 12.28) have an obligation to use them in God's service (whether within the church or without). 'By the grace of God, I am what I am,' says Paul, 'and his grace toward me was not in vain. On the contrary, I worked harder than any of them – though it was not I, but the grace of God which is with me' (1 Corinthians 15.10). All Paul's work would have been nothing without God's grace, but if he had neglected his calling, that grace would have been empty, 'in vain' (see 1 Corinthians 9.24–26).

106 By the same token, those who have the task of leadership discernment have an obligation to seek out and encourage God's gifting in others (see the instruction to Timothy to identify faithful teachers: 2 Timothy 2.2). Gifts can be neglected, buried in the ground, kept under wraps – or risked and put to work to bear fruit for the kingdom. Timothy is instructed (twice) not to neglect but to 'rekindle [fan into flames] the gift that is in you by the laying on of hands' (1 Timothy 1.14; 2 Timothy 1.6). Within the biblical understanding of leadership as gift, there is no room for undue self-importance ('What have you that you did not receive?', 1 Corinthians 4.6f). But there is plenty of space for obedience, grounded in love, as a proper response to the generosity of the Giver.

107 This is probably the best way to approach the thorny question of 'godly ambition'. The church has long worked with a model of modest reluctance in the pursuit of senior office, with the implication that the people most suited to office are almost by definition the least likely to seek it out. Is there a proper role for 'godly ambition' in the process of becoming a leader? We might perhaps more properly frame the question in terms of *aspiration*.[32] To aspire to *episkope* in the church of God is to

32 A term we owe to Fr Simon Holden CR.

desire 'a good work' according to 1 Timothy 3.1. Think of Paul's 'ambition to proclaim the good news' (Romans 15.20), and of his passionate longing ('divine jealousy') to present the Corinthian church to Christ 'as a pure bride to her husband' (2 Corinthians 11.2). In so far as such 'godly ambition' is for others (God's kingdom, Christ, the church,) not for oneself, it is never a matter for personal pride ('boasting'), but, equally, is not to be denied (2 Corinthians 10.7–8; 1 Corinthians 4.1–6).

108 It is, no doubt, a canny awareness of the almost infinite capacity of the human heart for self-deception that leads Paul to approach the subject of 'boasting' with a heavy amount of rhetorical irony (2 Corinthians 10–13). The developing church was clearly aware of the inherent potential for corruption in the discourse of leadership, and hedged it about with warnings (see James 3.1–2). Thus 1 Timothy 3.1–7 (the closest that the New Testament gets to a list of episcopal competencies) shows a clear awareness that the office carries with it the danger of being 'puffed up with conceit' (v.6). To counter this, the emphasis is on moral probity (vv.2–3), financial incorruptibility ('no lover of money'), proven management competence (vv. 4–5) and public accountability ('well thought of by outsiders', v.7). Such passages imply a presumption that those who love the Lord will love the church and therefore offer themselves for service within it.

109 The difficulty, then, becomes how to deal with an excess of motivation in wanting to take on church leadership. The tradition of expecting modest reluctance from those called to senior leadership (often described using the phrase *nolo episcopari*, 'I do not wish to be a bishop!') originated from that excess. The danger is that we internalise the tradition at a superficial level while losing the good desires that it was meant to channel and contain.

3.6 The ethos of leadership in the New Testament

110 We are now in a better position to attempt to sum up the distinctive ethos of leadership in the New Testament. The New Testament discourse of leadership shows a constant awareness of leadership as derived from God, refracted through the prism of divine leadership (the vertical axis) – and held in trust among and for others who are also called (the horizontal axis). New Testament writers show a constant readiness to adopt and adapt models from the secular world into the discourse of leadership – like the steward or household manager, reflecting the more domestic social context of the early church. But they are also constantly aware of the dangers of leadership: the dangers of pride, the dangers of power, the dangerous ideologies embedded in the discourse of leadership itself.

111 **Discipleship:** Leaders share the fundamental vocation of all Christians to discipleship. The first qualification for being a leader in the church is to be a follower. All leaders (lay and ordained) are those who have heard the call of Christ, who take seriously – however imperfectly – the transformative lifestyle of the Sermon on the Mount. They are open to a lifetime of learning, and committed to following Christ on the way of the cross. As with all disciples, their spiritual life is undergirded by the daily disciplines of prayer, attentiveness and obedience. As figures in the public eye, their personal commitment to probity (holiness) and the imitation of Christ has to be rooted in humility and integrity. Discipleship – the longing 'to be conformed to the image of God's Son' – is the undergirding aspiration that reaches out past the demands of a particular office, through a lifetime and beyond (Philippians 3.9–14).

112 **Charism:** Leaders share the anointing of all the baptised with the Holy Spirit. They recognise that leadership is a gift of the Holy Spirit, and, as members of the body of Christ, they exercise the particular gifts that equip them for leadership among and alongside other members whose diverse spiritual gifts need to be affirmed and encouraged. Those tasked with the selection and equipping of future leaders look for people already exercising spiritual gifts (both within the body of Christ and in the secular world).

113 Diakonia: Leadership is a *diakonia*, a ministry or 'commission', held in trust from God to be carried out in the service of others. Leaders share with other ministers an awareness of the givenness of ministry, a commitment to service and a sense of accountability. As a *diakonos Christi*, the leader is committed to a life of service, serving Christ by participating in his mission of service to the church and the world, and imitating the model of self-giving love displayed by Jesus himself. As faithful stewards of the mysteries of God (1 Corinthians 4.1), leaders are fellow-servants with the saints, serving the same master, tasked by the same Spirit with provisioning and resourcing the household of God (Matthew 24.45; Ephesians 4.12). They are commissioned to provision and support other ministers and disciples in their service in God's household, and are accountable to the Lord of the household (1 Corinthians 4.1–5). Their leadership is derived from and held in allegiance to God as the ultimate source of all authority. Hence leaders are repeatedly warned against 'acting the boss', usurping the authority that belongs to God alone (2 Corinthians 1.24; 1 Peter 5.3; Luke 22.25).[33]

114 Oversight (*episkope*): Nevertheless, leaders are called to exercise real authority – they have a calling that instils confidence both in the leader and in other members of the church. From earliest times, the church has sensed a need for order and focus, for a clarity of vision that looks to the needs of the whole body. This leadership is consensual. The social world of the New Testament

33 The same model of *diakonia* undergirds Paul's understanding of political authority in Romans 13, and is reflected in the prayers for the monarch in the 1662 *Book of Common Prayer.*

was intensely hierarchical; authority was instantly recognised and respected (Luke 7.8). It is all the more striking that leadership in the church is accorded by mutual recognition rather than imposed by external authority: it has to be 'recognised' (1 Corinthians 16.15, 1 Thessalonians 5.12). Effective leadership depends on co-operation between leaders and led (Hebrews 13.17; 1 Peter 5.2). It builds upon and extends the self-control and mutual oversight of the people. It is an *enabling* leadership, designed to support and build up; it is about 'power to' rather than 'power over'.[34] And it is a *representative* leadership: it is prepared to speak out, to offer advocacy on behalf of weaker members, to represent the community before the wider world.

115 Collegiality: Leadership is one manifestation of God's energy (literally 'in-working') in the life of the church (1 Corinthians 4.6). But leaders do not have a monopoly on that life-giving energy: they are aware that God is at work in many other individuals and other places in the life of the church (Philippians 2.12), and that theirs is but one of the gifts that God has given to the church. As such, it is never a solitary privilege: leadership is exercised in *collaboration* (Greek *synergy*) with others whose work is part of the same divine energy. Hence, church leadership in the New Testament is inherently *collegial*: both apostles and local leaders function as groups (or teams), rather than individuals. Jesus chose twelve apostles, not a single successor: collegiality is built into the model from the start. This collegiality is at the core of every level of the church's leadership, from the (sometimes tense) relationship between Paul and the Jerusalem apostles (Galatians 1–2) to the relationships within Paul's staff team and within local leadership teams.[35] Apostolic unity arises

---

34 Kathy Ehrensperger, *Paul and the Dynamics of Power: Communication and Interaction in the Early Christ-Movement*, London: T & T Clark, 2009.

35 This comes out particularly strongly in Paul's vocabulary describing his co-workers with a string of compounds beginning with the Greek prefix *sun-* ('with'): co-workers, fellow-prisoners, fellow-soldiers and so on.

not from monolithic structures of authority but from the containment of diversity and the negotiation of difference.

116 **Apostolicity**: The function of apostolicity is classically seen in the maintenance of continuity in the teaching ministry of the church. Crucial to the biblical concept of apostolicity is fidelity to the Jesus tradition: before the Gospels were written down, the apostles were the living chain of tradition that kept the church in touch with its Master, the ones who told the stories and maintained the memory that kept alive the scattered churches' umbilical link with Jesus. But this is not just about words or books: Integral to the apostolic lifestyle is *imitatio* or *mimesis*: the apostle is called first and foremost to model the Christ-like life, to be a living paradigm for a Spirit-filled life centred on the cross of Christ. To be an apostle is to be an agent, someone 'sent' to act on another's behalf. It gives you authority, but also responsibility (answerability) to your principal. Yet the apostles never act as agents of some global organisation called 'the church plc'; they are 'special agents' sent by Jesus Christ to act and speak and suffer on his behalf as his witnesses in the world. And this means being constantly thrown back to the ethos of leadership set by Jesus himself.

117 These themes converge in the dispute between the disciples over 'who should be called the greatest in the kingdom of heaven', recounted in Luke's Gospel (Luke 22.25–27). All the Gospels record, in one way or another, how Jesus responded to the tensions and ambitions latent in the disciple group by giving them some teaching on the nature of leadership. In John 13 this takes the form of the silent, acted parable of foot-washing, with the accompanying explanation: 'The servant (*doulos*) is not greater than the master (*kurios*), and the messenger (*apostolos*, i.e. one who is sent) is not greater than the sender' (John 13.16). John N. Collins is right to point out that the *diakonos* in Luke 22 functions exactly like the *apostolos* in John 13.16, drawing attention to the divine derivation of the messenger's authority, but it would be a gross misreading of the passage to miss the implied critique of hierarchy. The servant's authority is real: but it is also subordinate (Luke 22.27).[36] Those who exercise such authority have to be constantly vigilant not to fall into secular patterns of hegemony or to 'act the master' over those entrusted to their care.[38]

118 This scene (with its parallels) offers a dramatic representation of the New Testament ethos of leadership. On the horizontal axis, the apostles have to exercise their calling with and among others who owe allegiance to the same Lord (see John 21.20–23: 'What is that to you? Follow me!'). On the vertical axis, their leadership, like all human leadership, is derived from and subordinate to the leadership of the one Lord of the church; and their leadership style has to be modelled on that of the one who comes among us 'as one who serves'. Paul makes the same point in Philippians 2.1–11. To be a *diakonos Christou* is both an enormous privilege and enormously humbling; it is (to quote C.S. Lewis) 'both honour enough to erect the head of the poorest beggar, and shame enough to bow the shoulders of the greatest emperor on earth'.[36]

4 Faithful improvisation

119 The New Testament church does not provide us with a single model of leadership. Instead, it provides us with a fluid picture of ongoing adaptation, in which the divisions of ministry tasks between people and leaders, and between local and trans-local leaders, were re-negotiated in the light of changing circumstances and developing understanding, as was the nature of the task itself.

---

36 Contra Collins, *ho diakonon* here clearly carries the connotations of 'waiting at table' as well as the connotations of 'carrying out a commission' – the rhetoric of the sentence demands it. See further Alexander, '*Diakonia*, the Ephesian Comma, and the Ministry of All Believers'.

37 Compare Luke's *kurieuein* (Luke 22.25) with 1 Peter 5.3 (*katakurieuontes*).

38 C.S. Lewis, *Prince Caspian*, London: Collins, 1974, p. 191.

120 That negotiation took place between what Christians in any particular local context were *given*, and what they *found*. They were *given* the same commission to preach the gospel, to teach one another, to worship, to care for one another; they were given the same Lord, the same Spirit and the same Father, and a shared history of God's saving work. They *found* themselves, however, faced with very different circumstances: differing social settings, differing relationships to Jerusalem or to Rome, differing local cultures, in differing generations. They sought to do justice to these different situations (*locality*) while remaining recognisable to those in other locales (*catholicity*) and faithful to what they had inherited (*apostolicity*) – and that required of them creative and flexible improvisation.

121 In the process, they borrowed (as we have seen) language, ideas, practices and even forms of organisation from a wide variety of sources: the household, the estate, the empire and many other spheres of life. Some of these borrowings seem to have been quite deliberate, others were perhaps more unconscious, but they were pervasive and kaleidoscopic. As they sought to discover how to be faithful in their changing contexts, the Christians of the New Testament churches experimented with those borrowings in all sorts of imaginative ways, remaking them in the process. The story of their faithfulness is a story of creative borrowing and critical adaptation.

122 The subsequent history of Christian leadership, from the New Testament to today, continues this history of improvisation. At its best, it has been faithful improvisation: it has taken the themes and norms of the New Testament and Apostolic age, and sought to remain true to them, while at the same time adapting the methods, scope and organisation of church leadership to ensure that it served the Christian community effectively in changed conditions. This was never a one-way or one-dimensional matter, however. At different times, and in different places, different aspects of the New Testament picture would come to the fore, and then recede again.

123 The church, therefore, works creatively with the materials that it finds to hand, as it seeks to be faithful to what it has inherited. Precisely through this process, however, the Spirit can guide the church into deeper discovery of the nature of what it has received. That is, the process of faithful improvisation can itself, by God's gracious providence, become a means by which the church is shown the deeper structures of its faith. To describe the church's history of thought and practice in relation to leadership as a history of faithful improvisation does not, therefore, mean that this history is simply a succession of ephemeral experiments, each of no more value than the last. There is also a sense of cumulative, hard-won discovery – and we in our own improvisations are called to be faithful not simply to the original deposit of faith but to what the church has been shown about that faith by the Spirit in and through its history. This is why we turn from the biblical explorations of the previous chapter to the present chapter's explorations of Christian history.

124 We are not going to try to attempt even a bird's-eye overview of the whole history of this ongoing improvisation. A few unevenly scattered snapshots are all that we have space for, but we hope that they will be enough to show some of the kinds of adaptation and re-negotiation that have taken place, specifically (though not exclusively) in relation to episcopal leadership.[39]

4.1 The emergence of the three-fold order

125 It is within the leadership of the local church that we see the gradual emergence of the three-fold order of later centuries. Its

39 As part of the project, members of the Commission were asked to reflect on aspects of leadership in particular periods of church history. The following material is based on these more extended reflections, which are reproduced in Part 2 below.

roots (and its language) are already there in the New Testament. The deacon (*diakonos*: Romans 16.2; Philippians 1.1) and the *episkopos* or 'overseer' appear in Paul's undisputed letters, with *episkopoi* by implication the senior role (Philippians 1.1). The 'elder' (*presbyteros*) by definition implies seniority, both in the sense of physical age and of attributed honour (an assumption that creates problems for Timothy's 'youth': 1 Timothy 4.12). The term was already current in contemporary social life, both Jewish and Greek, and appears as a Christian office in Acts and the later epistles.[40] What is unclear (and remains so throughout the first two centuries) is the structural relationship between these two 'senior' offices: most scholars now accept that the two terms were used concurrently in different parts of the Christian world, and only slowly amalgamated into a single system.[41] But both terms attest to the existence and importance of 'senior leadership' within the local church, amongst a still flexible and burgeoning array of local ministries.

126 At this stage, then, *episkope* was exercised both in the local church (by the local presbyter-bishops) and at trans-local level (by the apostles). The *episkopoi* belonged firmly within the leadership of the local church; it was the apostles who represented the third 'order of ministry'. Within the local church, we can begin to see a gradual shift from a two-fold order of *presbyteroi* and *diakonoi* (Titus) to a three-fold order where one of the *presbyteroi* was singled out as *episkopos* with some kind of supervisory role or 'oversight' over the rest (1 Timothy 3.1ff). But there is no sign that the *episkopos* had taken over the role of the itinerant apostle: that still belonged to Paul and his travelling team. What is missing

40 Titus 1.5; 1 Timothy 5.17; 1 Peter 5.1–5; James 5.14; 3 John; Acts 11.30, 14.23, 15.2–16.4, 20.17, 21.18.

41 As Gregory Dix observes, as late as AD 200 'it is exceedingly difficult to relate the presbyterate to the episcopate and diaconate as elements in a single organization' (in 'The Ministry in the Early Church', in Kirk, *Apostolic Ministry*, pp. 183–304, at p. 222). On the office of elder, see R. Alistair Campbell, *The Elders: Seniority within Earliest Christianity*, Edinburgh: T & T Clark, 1994; Roger Beckwith, *Elders in Every City: The Origin and Role of the Ordained Ministry*, Carlisle: Paternoster, 2003; and Stewart, *Original Bishops*, ch. 4, and the literature cited there.

(to our eyes) is a management structure to link the two forms of *episkope*. Both exercised authority, and sometimes they came into conflict (as, for example, in Paul's relationship with the church in Corinth). But for the most part the two forms of authority worked together, in a partnership (*koinonia*: Paul's preferred word for his relationship with the Philippians) of mutual checks and balances.

127 The real crunch came in the last decades of the first century, with the death of the apostolic generation. The later books of the New Testament (Acts, Hebrews and 1 Peter) stand at this point, and show a concern for the future training and validation of the local leadership. One way to secure this was to demonstrate an 'apostolic succession' by making explicit the endorsement and training of local leaders that is implicit in the core epistles.[42] The Pastoral Epistles show a similar set of concerns: Paul in prison, facing death, is concerned about false teaching, managing and organising his team, and preparing them to carry on without him. In 1 Timothy and Titus we see this delegation in action, creating an apostolic link to the elders of the local churches via Timothy and Titus and offering a very specific set of instructions for leadership training.

128 Thus, even within the New Testament we can see fluidity and development – 'faithful improvisation' – in the structures of leadership within the church: structures that vary and evolve, under the guidance of the Spirit, to meet the challenges of new situations. It is no coincidence that the period after the death of the apostles saw the *episkopoi* of the local church gradually assuming a more 'apostolic' role. To the historian, this was essentially a contingent and human historical process, responding to changing circumstances. But that does not mean that such contingent and human processes are outside the

42 See Gregory Dix's section 'On the development of the idea of apostolic succession' in 'Ministry in the Early Church', pp. 201–13.

providence of God. They can be seen as a recognition of and response to an essentially theological perception: that the well-being of the church, its right ordering under God, demands both local leadership and the kind of trans-local leadership provided by the apostles. Indeed, the Anglican Church (among others) teaches that the emergence of the three-fold order is one of those discoveries about the deep structure of the faith into which the Spirit has led the church. The church, Anglicans have said, needs episcopal, priestly and diaconal ministry in order to be fully itself, and this is an abiding insight into the nature of the church to which we, in our own ongoing improvisations, are called to respond.

4.2 The historic episcopate

129 Thus the historic episcopate in its classic form stands at the confluence of the two strands of leadership we saw in the New Testament: the local and the apostolic. In the post-apostolic period there was a gradual shift in the balance between 'local' and 'trans-local' leadership, and a bid to capture the trans-local teaching authority of the apostles for the local *episkopoi*. This came about quite slowly and piecemeal over the second and third centuries – a multifaceted renegotiation of the triangular pattern we have seen in the New Testament period, involving complex gains and losses.[43]

130 One result was a re-definition of *locality*. The *episkopoi* in effect remained local church leaders, but the definition of 'locality' enlarged and solidified from the house-church to the city and eventually its surrounding region (*dioikesis*). With this growth in scale came an ever-greater structural complexity, requiring growing numbers of subordinate clergy to assist the bishop in

43 The *Didache* (ch. 11) is revealing here: there are still itinerant 'prophets and apostles', who are treated with residual respect but also with a marked degree of suspicion; priestly tithes are to be given to local teachers. (See 'Didache' in Michael W. Holmes (ed.), *The Apostolic Fathers: Greek Texts and English Translations,* 3rd edn, Grand Rapids, MI: Baker Academic, 2007, pp. 344–69.)

his role. The deacons of this period were essentially the bishop's personal staff (with the role of archdeacon emerging within this structure). The role of presbyter evolved from a collegial structure (individual house-church leaders meeting as a collegial body on a city-wide basis) to a more hierarchical one (presbyters as delegates and surrogates for a monarchical bishop). Nevertheless, aspects of the older patterns (such as the collegial role of the presbyters) survived (and still survive) in the rites of ordination. And the symbolic importance of locality in the authority of the bishop endured in the continuing practice of the bishop's election by the people throughout the pre-Nicene period.[44]

131 At the same time we find a process of *centralisation of ministries* within the local church. The episcopate gradually drew into itself the striking variety of ministry tasks found in the Pauline churches. Ministry tasks that had once (in those churches) been undertaken by a variety of church members came to be regarded as the preserve of a growing clerical elite. Eventually a concept of local *monarchia* began to emerge, which in time marginalised all other forms of spiritual authority within the bishop's *provincia* – prophetic, ascetic and patronal authority (including the authority of women). This was all part of a process of clericalisation which drew an increasingly strong distinction between 'laity' and 'clergy' (terms that are hardly applicable in the New Testament period). Here we see the beginnings of 'a clear trajectory that renders the laity ever more passive and gives ever higher standing to the clergy'.[45]

132 Thus the episcopate combines within itself two forms of leadership: the mobile, missionary, trans-local leadership of the apostles; and the stable, locally rooted (and locally accountable) leadership of the local *episkopoi*. As *local* leaders,

44 Cf. Dix, 'Ministry in the Early Church', pp. 198–9.

45 Karen Jo Torjesen, 'Clergy and Laity', in Susan A. Harvey and David G. Hunter (eds), *The Oxford Handbook of Early Christian Studies*, Oxford: Oxford University Press, 2008, pp. 389–405, at p. 401.

the bishops inherit the tasks of the local *episkopoi*, taking responsibility for the community's worship (presiding at the Eucharist); for moral discipline and spiritual growth within the community; and for the community's extensive charitable work among the poor. Episcopal leadership grew organically out of the hospitality and patronage of local house-church hosts, which included taking responsibility for providing premises and resources for the community meal, as well as the patronal role of offering advocacy and support within the wider community. As the church grew, the task got bigger, but it was essentially the same task. There is a direct line of continuity from Justin's 'president' handing out food parcels at the Eucharist to Basil's full-sized hospital complex.[46]

133 But the office of the bishop also inherits the mantle of *apostolic* leadership. This gives it the essential dimension of *catholicity*, setting the episcopate (and the local church) firmly within the setting of the wider church. Apostolic leadership took responsibility for the mission of the church in preaching and apologetic to the wider world, and, crucially, for the memory of the church – for keeping the church in touch with the words and work of Jesus. Thus the apostolic task of teaching came to assume an increasingly central place in the role of the bishop, especially in defining the boundaries between orthodoxy and heresy (Ignatius, Irenaeus). The early church was primarily defined by its ideology rather than nationality or geography (though it reverted to more traditional factors like race and place later as the church becomes normalised in society). This necessitated teachers to communicate that ideology because there was no other way for Christianity to pass from one generation to the next. Continuity with the original 'apostolic' teaching and model of leadership remains an essential part of

46 Justin, *First Apology*, 67.6–7. On Basil, see P.J. Fedwick, *The Church and the Charisma of Leadership in Basil of Caesarea*, Toronto: Pontifical Institute of Medieval Studies, 1979.

how the church identifies itself – and thus an essential aspect of senior leadership – into the present day.

134 This fact in itself precipitated a change in the identity and authority of the *episkopoi*: 'as soon as *teaching* becomes essential to the role, wealth and patronage are no longer sufficient qualifications'.[47] Already in the New Testament a double measure of 'honour' was accorded to elders who teach as well as 'rule'.[48] Increasingly, as the church grew in social status and influence, it had to find senior leaders who benefited from a classical education in rhetoric (the theory and practice of persuasive public speaking). They had to be educated in order to engage with the world of non-Christians all around them. They were well used to countering (in speech or writing) the attacks of non-Christians on the intelligibility of Christianity. It is evident that such leaders were expected to be men of intellectual, moral and spiritual stature. What is less often understood is that they needed to be communicators who were also persuaders.

135 Thus, as the church grew in size and social standing, its leadership grew to match. The essential ministry tasks remained the same but the church needed leaders who could cope with social change and operate in the new, wider world that was opening up: bishops who were also politicians, like Ambrose, John Chrysostom and Athanasius; and bishops who were theologians before all else, like Augustine and Gregory of Nyssa.

136 Our documents tend to focus on those who fit the ancient 'type' of a leader in terms of birth and background, education and character, privileging adult males without physical defect and of a certain moral and spiritual character (which the ancient

47 Stewart, *Original Bishops*, p. 164.

48 1 Timothy 5.17. Stewart is almost certainly correct here to read *time* as the 'honour' accorded to a generous patron, not the 'pay' offered to a subordinate officer: Stewart, *Original Bishops*, pp. 147–64.

world conceived as 'fixed' rather than developing). They privilege the kinds of leader which their – and our – cultural mythology and history prefer: heroes, people of stature, of moral courage or sharp intellect. They also shape the messy reality of individual leaders' actions into familiar moral types, to ease this process of interpretation and prioritisation.

4.3 Monks and martyrs

137 Meanwhile, however, new ways of accruing public authority for the exercise of different kinds of leadership are beginning to emerge in society in the fourth century. Peter Brown's work on the figure of the 'Holy Man' in late Antiquity shows how the lone ascetic, dedicated to the pursuit of holiness and the service of God, could come to exercise (without seeking it) a localised form of spiritual leadership 'on the ground'.[49] The increasing prestige associated with asceticism privileged those who had proven their worth by undergoing physical privations either willingly as monastics or forcibly as confessors (that is, those who have demonstrated their willingness to suffer as martyrs). The consecrated virgin carried considerable moral and spiritual authority by reason of her 'purity', and could therefore intervene in public affairs.[50] The authority of wives and sisters was not to be despised either: Christian women like Helena, Eudoxia, Faustina and Justina all exercised leadership in church and imperium – as did Macrina in a different sphere.[51] But their authority derived from their selves, the combining of a personality and character with a role and situation, without

49 Peter Brown, 'The Rise and Function of the Holy Man in Late Antiquity', *Journal of Roman Studies* 61 (1971), pp. 80–101.

50 Marina Warner, *Alone of All Her Sex: The Myth and Cult of the Virgin Mary*, 2nd edn, London: Pan Books, 1985, esp. pp. 50–67.

51 See Kate Cooper, *Band of Angels: The Forgotten World of Early Christian Women*, London: Atlantic, 2013, ch. 7.

any support from the traditional male sources of leadership legitimation (army, priesthood, legislature).

138 The history of early monasticism very clearly takes the form of a series of experiments in faithfulness, with each rule a distinct improvisation, giving rise to its own evolving tradition of ongoing improvisations, through the medieval period and beyond. One particularly influential text (both now and then) was the *Rule of St Benedict*. The Rule recalls the 'triangular' pattern of leadership we identified in the New Testament. The abbot's authority is significantly (and systematically) qualified or constrained. In principle, he commands obedience only as one himself under obedience, and insofar as he points away from himself to Christ: 'The authority of the abbot has nothing in it which is of itself; it is oriented to the realisation of the purpose of the rule which is to lead a community in the school of discipleship to be conformed to the passion of Christ; its purpose is to foster and nurture the making holy of Christian sinners. He is not to give way to his own preferences (RB 64) and he is under the same commitment to renounce his own will as his fellow monks. The object is the good and flourishing of the monks, whether strong or weak. Indeed he is to give attention to the individual needs and peculiarities as much as to the general requirements of the community's life, adapting himself to the ways of the monks (RB 2.31). The authority of the abbot may be called a supple authority.'[52]

139 Above all, the abbot is not a substitute for Christ, even if there is an evocation of the relationship of disciples to Christ in the relationship of the community to the abbot, and in their response to the abbot's commands and teaching, a response which is treated under the term 'obedience'. The abbot is a servant (*servus*) or rather fellow-servant (RB 64.13) with the

---

52 Xavier McMonagle O.S.B., 'The Service of Authority: The Abbot in the Rule of Benedict', *Cistercian Studies* 17 (1982), pp. 316–37.

members of the community, who are also *servi,* all serving the same Lord and all directed to the same end. The abbot is bound to consult – and, moreover, to consult the youngest, the most recently admitted of the members (RB 3). All members of the community are called to participate in weighty decisions affecting the community because God often reveals what is better to the younger members. After listening to all the members, Benedict gives the final decision to the abbot but it is unusual for an abbot to decide against the community's choice. Indeed, modern church law requires some decisions to be made by the chapter, rather than the abbot alone. Capacity to direct is shaped by the life of the community: 'The abbot's power is limited by the reality of the life.'[53]

140 These monastic ideas and practices of Christ-focused rule and obedience filtered back into the wider church, and helped shape evolving ideas of episcopal authority – providing one powerful set of lenses through which to understand the triangle of relationships between God, leader and people. Particularly influential was the *Pastoral Rule* of Gregory the Great (itself heavily dependent on the *Rule of St Benedict*), which became something of a guidebook in the Western Middle Ages for bishops, abbots and Christian monarchs alike. The overlap it presumes between being a pastor and being a ruler in the context of Christendom indicates that 'transferability' of leadership skills is not an idea wholly without precedent in Christian tradition.

141 Gregory's *Pastoral Rule* begins by defining the particular character of Christian pastoral responsibility (as we might put it) in terms of its goal: that it seeks to prepare people for the vision of God by fostering their growth in the virtues. From that starting point, Gregory focuses on two particular areas

---

53 Rembert Weakland O.S.B., 'Obedience to the Abbot and the Community in the Monastery', *Cistercian Studies* 5 (1970), pp. 309–16, at p. 315.

that follow naturally enough. The first is the need for the person who exercises such responsibility to be wholly committed to this goal in their own life, and to remain committed enough to cope with the inevitable distractions and temptations that such office will bring in its train. Importance is also given to a collegial approach to life and decision-making, including the election of a new abbot by the community and the abbot living among the community. In this context, we might say, leadership in the church requires a decision to seek continuing transformation in company with those whom it seeks to lead towards the common goal of the face of God.

142 The second area is the need for continual wisdom and discernment as the pastor-ruler communicates day by day with all manner of people in all manner of situations, so as to speak the word that these particular men and women need to hear at this particular time in order to move forward in their discipleship. Leadership in the church, in Gregory's account, requires a kind of constant 'faithful improvisation' from the rich resources of Scripture and traditions of prayerful reflection on it.

4.4 Monasteries and mission

143 We often talk as if there were an unbroken line of development from the structures of the post-Constantinian (or more properly post-Theodosian) imperial church to the self-confident affluence of the medieval episcopacy. In fact, the centuries after Constantine saw the break-up of the old Roman civic order across Europe and the rise of new and powerful, often tribal, societies. New forms of leadership were required to deal with a new situation. The monastic tradition played a significant role in the survival and spread of Christianity across Western Europe. Monasteries offered security in a disintegrating world; they preserved classical teaching and used it to shape a new Christian culture. And they formed the nodes of a new Christian network, increasingly centred on Rome. The story of how

Christianity spread across the British Isles is vividly told in Bede's *History of the English Church and People*. Bede's work also reflects another tradition, often known as Celtic, which encouraged a view that the primary responsibility of bishops was to oversee, lead and enable effective mission.[54] This was a responsibility both for the direction and co-ordination of the Christian community and for strategic Christian relations and communications with the wider culture, and it was based in a disciplined and collegial life of prayer.

144 The Celtic church was structured around bishops who were also abbots. The abbot-bishop was the chief strategist and enabler who sent apostles, often themselves bishops, 'on mission'. In the seventh century the Roman mission to Wessex was led by a Benedictine bishop, Birinus, who became the abbot-bishop at Dorchester. Later the abbot-bishop model was amalgamated with the Latin model in Anglo-Saxon Wessex with the transfer of Birinus' seat to the See of Winchester.[55] The monastic rule of life was a vital resource for mission. There were ongoing cross-cultural missions within and beyond the British Isles, including Patrick to Ireland, Aidan to northern Britain, Boniface to Germany, and many more. Another stream flowed from monasteries of England to the Scandinavian countries, where English monks, either as simple missionaries or as bishops and royal protégés, helped Christianise the north.[56]

145 Bede's account of St Chad clarifies the missionary focus of these early bishops: 'As a bishop, Chad immediately devoted himself to maintain the truths of the church, and set himself to practise humility and continence, and to study. After the example of the

54 See John Finney, *Recovering the Past: Celtic and Roman Mission*, London: DLT, 1996.

55 The conversion of Britain was not a simple matter, but was nevertheless a profound one that reached the depths of culture and helped forge a new cultural identity. See Barbara Yorke, *The Conversion of Britain: Religion, Politics and Society in Britain 600–800*, Harlow: Longman, 2006.

56 David Knowles, *The Monastic Order in England*, Cambridge: Cambridge University Press, 1963, pp. 46, 67–9.

Apostles, he travelled on foot and not on horseback when he went to preach the Gospel, whether in towns, the countryside, cottages, villages, or castles, for he was one of Aidan's disciples and always sought to instruct his people by the same methods as Aidan and his own brother Cedd.'[57] When Chad became Bishop of Lichfield (then a huge area stretching from the Trent to the Scottish borders), he continued to pursue the same simple but effective pattern he had learned from Aidan, an approach that almost got him into trouble with his new archbishop: 'The most reverend Bishop Chad always preferred to undertake his preaching missions on foot rather than on horseback, but Theodore ordered him to ride whenever he undertook a long journey. He was most reluctant to forgo this pious exercise, which he loved, but the archbishop, who recognised his outstanding holiness and considered it more proper for him to ride, himself insisted on helping him to mount his horse.'[58] The image of the missionary bishop, covering the huge areas of his diocese on horseback, irresistibly recalls the missionary travels of John Wesley.

4.5 Leadership in the Reformation

146 There is a sense in which the Reformation could be interpreted as the ultimate crisis in church leadership. Many of the questions that drove the Reformation centred around issues which, in the twenty-first century, we would categorise as leadership. Who had responsibility for the pastoral care and the teaching of the people in any given place? Who determined appointments in a parish or to a diocese? Who was responsible for providing structures and instruction that would support the spiritual health of the people of God? In different places, or in the same

---

57 Bede, *A History of the English Church and People*, tr. Leo Sherley-Price, London: Penguin, 1968, 3.28.

58 Bede, *History* 4.2.

place at different times, answers to these questions might include, variously, the bishop of the diocese, the city council, a local prince or ruler, the pope, the king or the emperor. The Reformation saw a very wide variety of experiments in reformulating the role of bishops or other senior leaders. Bishops became (among many other things) reformers and inspectors of preaching, and leaders of the education of their clergy. The division between local and trans-local leaders, the relationship between leaders and people, and the responsibilities of all these to God were all re-thought with a new centrality given to the ministry of the word.

147 Fundamental to the cluster of reform movements we call 'the Reformation' was the rediscovery of the laity. Luther was convinced that spiritual authority lay not only with clergy but with the whole people of God: therefore, he concluded, 'it is the duty of every Christian to espouse the cause of the faith, to understand and defend it, and to denounce every error'.[59] Luther's conviction that every believer stood equal before God, and that all believers were called to propagate gospel truth, has come to be known as the doctrine of the priesthood of all believers. However, although he was convinced that every Christian had a role to play in the propagation of gospel truth, he was nonetheless adamant that a specific (and indeed male) person must be appointed to preach the gospel and celebrate the sacraments in the context of parish worship. As he explained in his lectures on Titus, 'Christians all have a priesthood, but they do not all have the priestly function. Although all can teach and exhort, nevertheless one ought to do so, and the others ought to listen.'[60] The common priesthood shared by all believers did not mandate all Christians to a public ministry.

---

59 Martin Luther, 'To the Christian Nobility of the German Nation', tr. Charles M. Jacobs, *Three Treatises*, Philadelphia: Fortress Press, 1990, p. 22.

60 Luther, Lectures on *Titus, Philemon & Hebrews*, tr. Walter A. Hansen, Luther's Works 29, St Louis, MI: Concordia, 1968, p. 17.

The appropriate leadership of the church included the discernment of the proper tasks of bishops and priests, and the establishment of structures that would enable them to carry out those tasks without distraction.

148 The reformers also had a strong sense of the importance of *locality*. Luther argued that local clergy should be appointed with some attention to the local community: 'When a bishop consecrates [someone as a parish priest] it is nothing else than that in the place and stead of the whole community, all of whom have like power, he takes a person and charges him to exercise this power on behalf of the others.'[61] Though bishops might, at least in theory, be appointed to the oversight of a larger area, the nature of pastoral oversight required that these bishops or elders (who, in Luther's view, might better be termed 'inspectors' or 'visitors') should know their people well enough to exhort them to a better life: 'Every city ought to have many bishops, that is, inspectors or visitors. Such an inspector should be the parish clergyman along with the chaplain, so that they may share the duties and see how people live and what is taught. He would see who is a usurer, and then he would speak the Word of healing and correction.'[62] This concern for the locality of oversight re-surfaces a century later in Richard Baxter's *Reformed Pastor*: 'When we are commanded to take heed to all the flock, it is plainly implied, that flocks must ordinarily be no greater than we are capable of overseeing, or "taking heed" to.'[63]

149 One solution to this problem (favoured by the more radical groups) was to reform the *structures* of senior leadership. In seventeenth-century England the issue, as Judith Maltby argues,

---

61 Luther, 'To the Christian Nobility', p. 128.

62 Luther, *Lectures on Titus*, p. 17.

63 Richard Baxter, *The Reformed Pastor*, first published in 1656; cited from the abridged edition, Edinburgh: Banner of Truth Trust, 1997, ch. II, sect.1: 'The nature of this oversight'.

was a fundamental difference over the shape of church order.[64] Presbyterians and Episcopalians agreed that every local church or congregation should have its own pastor, and both cited in their favour the New Testament pattern of 'elders in every town'. What the Presbyterians contested was the distortion of this essentially 'flat' picture of church order by the elevation of the bishop to a higher order.

150 However, most of the reformers sought not so much to abolish the episcopate as to restore it to its biblical roots. Bishops, in Erasmus' view, had lost sight of the true function of the office – the preaching and teaching of Scripture, and the administration of the sacraments – had forgotten their responsibility to pursue a holy life, and had become caught up in the intricacies of worldly politics and concerns. They were not, in any proper sense, spiritual leaders. Erasmus' critique would be echoed by Martin Luther. The two men were part of a mood of anti-clericalism which was united (if not always fair) in its denouncement of the immorality and spiritual incompetence of the church's leaders. For them the issue was not so much the structures of *episkope* as a return to its proper tasks and ethos: the ministry of word and sacrament, the care of the poor and the diligent pastoral oversight of every soul under their care.

151 The Church of England's decision to retain the historic three-fold order of bishop, priest and deacon also reflects the political realities of the Reformation in England. Luther would have been very glad to enlist the bishops on the side of Reform – if only he could have found any bishops willing to support him.[65] In England, the situation was rather different. Where Luther

64 Judith Maltby, *Prayer Book and People in Elizabethan and Early Stuart England,* Cambridge: Cambridge University Press, 2000, p. 160.

65 Wendebourg, 'Reformation in Germany'. For Sir Thomas Aston, this was an example of the ambivalence of the reformers' position: 'It was with palpable pleasure that Aston provided evidence that Calvin's views on the Episcopal office were not abstract absolutes but changed to reflect actual circumstances.' (Maltby, *Prayer Book and People*, pp. 158–9).

struggled to find political support from the imperial princes and bishops, the Reformation in England could claim a distinguished series of bishops among its martyrs. And the Reformation found an unlikely political ally in Henry VIII. Having displaced the Pope as head of the Church in England, Henry (and his successors) *needed* bishops as part of the fabric of government.[64] Episcopacy and monarchy were always closely intertwined in England ('no bishop, no king') and became even more so in the pre-Civil War period as Charles I, aided and abetted by Archbishop Laud, sought to govern without Parliament. Thus it was more or less inevitable that, after the Civil War, the restoration of episcopacy went hand in hand with the restoration of the monarchy.

152 Thus, in the early modern period, as 'Lords Spiritual' bishops remained powerful figures in the Court and in Parliament, whose authority depended not only on a coherent theological understanding of the relationship of ministry and gospel but also on their position near the summit of the social hierarchy. Even when modestly born (and many were, until the mid-eighteenth century), their general literary and social abilities, allied to their ecclesiastical status, made them central to the particular configuration of church and state that held sway until the constitutional revolution of the mid-nineteenth-century Reform era.

4.6 Leadership in the nineteenth and twentieth centuries

153 The seamless alliance between secular and ecclesiastical leadership remained a striking feature of senior leadership in

---

66 John Findon, 'Developments in the Understanding and Practice of Episcopacy in the Church of England', in Dalferth and Hoare, *Visible Unity and the Ministry of Oversight*, pp. 79–92.

the Church of England right through to the mid-twentieth century. David Edwards, in his study of *Leaders of the Church of England, 1828–1978*, remarks on their conspicuous assurance 'in what they commonly took for granted ... A whole complex of privileges combined to give them this pride in belonging to their Church and civilisation ... They were all the sons of Christian homes, with their basic values clear from the beginning. Almost all of them were educated in strong Anglican schools [and] at Oxford and Cambridge. Their domestic circumstances were usually easy; they had servants [and supportive wives] even while they were parish priests or schoolmasters. When they talked or preached, they expected others to listen and learn. In their teaching they appealed to the authority of the Bible, reinforced by the authority of a Christian consensus which had shaped England for more than a thousand years. In discharging their administrative responsibilities in school or college, parish or diocese, nation or empire, they felt themselves to be members of a governing class, close to the Crown; and their fellow-rulers accepted them, inviting them to dinner, enquiring after their opinions, complimenting their ladies, mourning their deaths. They were solid figures in the English Establishment, and the English Establishment was then dominant over national, and much of international, life.'[67] Even at the end of the Second World War, he adds, 'it was possible to retain the illusion that nothing had really changed'.

154 Yet the intimations of change were already visible in the nineteenth century, for those who had eyes to see. Their social influence increasingly challenged, the bishops and other church leaders sought to reinvigorate ecclesiastical administration. Many bishops became busy municipal administrators, exercising a paternalistic rule over a whole diocese – another in a long

67 David L. Edwards, *Leaders of the Church of England, 1828–1978*, London: Hodder & Stoughton, 1978, pp. 350f.

line of reformulations of their public role. At the same time, thanks to the Oxford Movement, there was another rethinking of the whole triangle of relationships, now with a new centrality given to sacramental ministry.

155 The term 'leadership' was almost never used of a bishop in this period, yet the rise of a conception of bishop's 'rule' reflected a new-found confidence in their intrinsic spiritual authority. But concepts of 'rule' could never last long in a time of unprecedented social and economic change. The democratic, reforming tide that swept aside the old Anglican constitutional hegemony also eroded traditional assumptions about social hierarchy. When state subsidies for church-building ceased, the church rate was abolished, Parliament was opened to Dissenters, Roman Catholics, Jews and atheists, and the ecclesiastical courts were largely bypassed, bishops could, in fact, no longer 'rule': they had to argue, persuade and, above all, lead by example. They became, to all intents and purposes, much like the leaders of other voluntary organisations, albeit with much more than a residuum of traditional paraphernalia.

156 One of the most significant developments in the Church of England in the twentieth century was the re-awakening of the laity. As the laity started to gain a significant voice (both in parochial church councils and subsequently through the adoption of a synodical system of government), clergy had to learn new ways of exercising leadership. That, in turn, opened up the Church of England to new challenges, at a time when resources began to be threatened. The improvisations of the twentieth and twenty-first centuries are all around us – the huge increase and diversification of lay involvement, lay ministry and lay leadership in the church; various forms of team ministry involving new ways of handling collegiality; the emergence of secular management roles within diocesan and cathedral structures, involving a new division of labour in senior leadership; and many others.

157 Behind all these, and shaping contemporary notions of what church leaders actually do, were accompanying developments in church bureaucracy and management. Some have described these as part of a process of professionalisation, though to what extent this is an adequate description is open to dispute. From the mid-twentieth century, bishops and others were indeed beginning to use the language of 'leadership', not as a simple theft from the secular world of management theory but as a useful term for naming the many skills of negotiation, consultation and organisation they had to deploy to help chart the church's course in a time of shrinking membership, growing religious pluralism and (most recently) new legal responsibilities in terms of safeguarding children and vulnerable adults.

158 Alongside these rapid changes in the role of senior clergy, new forms of Christian leadership began to spring up alongside traditional church structures. David Edwards' study includes influential lay leaders like Gladstone, Wilberforce and Shaftesbury alongside bishops and archbishops. These great nineteenth-century social reformers, driven by the imperative of 'doing the gospel', provided a form of Christian leadership in society that conspicuously superseded formal clergy–lay distinctions. This was also the period of the great pan-evangelical mission societies, intentional communities, networks and agencies, which operated with an 'essentially pragmatic' approach to leadership and offered new ways of handling the trans-local dimension of Christian leadership. They 'sought and acquired influential patronage, mobilised mass support by constructing a network of local auxiliary societies, and co-operated with any who shared their aims regardless of belief',[68] making a positive virtue of combining ecclesiastical, civic and business leadership in interdenominational projects, societies and councils.

---

68 Doreen Rosman, *Evangelicals and Culture*, 2nd edn, London: James Clarke, 2012, p. 17.

159 This pan-evangelical activism, and the generic leadership paradigms which accompanied it, saw a resurgence in the second half of the twentieth century, from the Billy Graham crusades of the 1950s and '60s, to the socially-active campaigning organisations such as TEAR Fund, CARE for the Family, Christians in Parliament, the AIDS charity ACET and many more.[69] Many of the most influential evangelical leaders of the late twentieth century came out of such trans-local networks operating above and behind the formal structures of parish and diocese – ranging from the elitist V.P.S. 'Bash camps', through the Church Growth strategists of the 1980s, to the 'Executive Archpastor' (David Hilborn's term) who operates as CEO of a large and successful church, becoming 'less and less of a pastor to individuals and more and more simply the supervisor and eventually the manager of a network of pastoral carers and other systems'.[70]

160 These movements are often led by Christian businesspeople who are more at home with the language and operating methods of business 'leadership' than with the traditional categories of the church. They have been highly successful in training generations of Christian leaders. Yet, for all the biblical teaching and discipleship training they offer, it is still noticeable that they sometimes operate with a relatively uncritical acceptance of secular hierarchy and power. In this sense, they are prone to similar hermeneutical criticism as might be levelled at unfiltered application of secular management, business or civic paradigms of leadership – or at the 'worldliness' of the medieval bishops.

---

69 Tim Chester, *Awakening to a World of Need: Recovery of Evangelical Social Concern*, Leicester: IVP, 1993; Ian Randall and David Hilborn, *One Body in Christ: The History and Significance of the Evangelical Alliance*, Carlisle: Paternoster, 2001, pp. 208–82.

70 Croft, *Ministry in Three Dimensions*, p. 24.

4.7 The nature of improvisation

161 These are only very brief snapshots of a complex history, but they are perhaps sufficient to demonstrate a number of important points.

162 The most obvious point is that change is not a new experience for the church. It simply is not the case that earlier generations enjoyed an unvarying stability in the idea and practice of senior leadership, or that it is only we in the early twenty-first century who are facing upheavals and transformations. In the context of church history as a whole, our time is not a time of greater change, nor a time of greater complexity – it is simply a time of *different* change and *different* complexity. We should not, therefore, think in terms of a conflict between a single, stable, 'inherited' model of leadership and our dramatic new developments (whether we use that contrast to praise the old or the new). Rather, we stand within an ongoing history of improvisation, and are called to continue it and (where we believe that the Spirit has revealed more of God's abiding will for the church through this history) to build on it. We are called to improvise faithfully in our own time too.

163 Something else follows from this. If, looking back, we can see how complex the interaction has always been between models of leadership and the social conditions in which they have been exercised, we must be especially careful not to oversimplify our understanding of the world in which we find ourselves now. It is very unlikely that there exists a model of church leadership today that can address decisively *all* of the challenges the Church of England faces. But at the same time the church must study those challenges closely, and look carefully at the many different contexts and circumstances in which leadership is wanted.

164 It is also clearly impossible to sustain a simple opposition between Christian and secular ideas of leadership. Our tradition has always been in the business of assimilating and transforming material from the world around it. Ultimately, all the language we use about leadership – whether we say ‘bishop’ or ‘leader’, ‘shepherd’ or ‘counsellor’, ‘servant leader’ or ‘deacon’, ‘prince’ or ‘priest’ or ‘elder’ – is language that has been borrowed, assimilated and transformed. The only interesting questions are about the kind and depth of the transformation and assimilation involved, not about the fact of borrowing itself.

165 Of course, some of our language about leadership has a very long history of churchly appropriation and re-appropriation, and so has come to seem like it is firmly ‘our language’ – but none of it, even so, has achieved absolute finality and stability. What we mean by ‘pastor’ now is not identical to what we might have meant by ‘pastor’ 50 or 100 or 400 years ago. That word, like all the words we use, has picked up new connotations and had old connotations rubbed off as it has been used in our changing contexts, and so it stands in need of thoughtful testing, of critical appropriation, just as much as words freshly picked up from contexts outside the church. On the other hand, it is, of course, true that much of the language we have picked up more recently has not yet been well assimilated (like the idea of a church leader as a CEO), and some may prove to be all but inassimilable.

166 We should not, therefore, assume any neat opposition between theological and secular, nor between traditional and innovative ideas of leadership. Rather, we need to focus on the process of critical appropriation or negotiation: the process by which we bring all our languages and practices of leadership, wherever they come from and however long we have inhabited them, before the God who calls us and commissions us, to be transformed and remade. After all, ‘traditional’ language and ideas can become a way of protecting ourselves against such necessary transformation, just as much as new language borrowed from the wider world can distract us from it. Yet newly borrowed language can serve to drive us more deeply into our faith, in unexpected and refreshing ways, just as much as traditional language can call us to remember our deepest responsibilities and help us keep hold of the hard-won wisdom discovered and tested in earlier negotiations of the church.

5 Facing the future

167 We began with three questions.

- Is it right to make 'leadership' a central idea in the life of the church?
- If so, what are the underlying theological principles that inform the exercise of leadership within the church?
- How can these principles best inform the exercise of senior leadership in the Church of England today?

168 We can now give a more precise answer to the first of these questions. It can only be right to make 'leadership' a central idea in the life of the church if our ideas and practices of leadership (whether inherited from earlier generations of the church or borrowed from elsewhere) are subjected to ongoing critical questioning in the light of the church's relation to its Lord. A simple 'yes' or 'no' answer to this question threatens to bypass that critical questioning, and should be avoided.

169 As for the second and third questions, we can now give them a new formulation. We are asking: *What faithful improvisations upon the traditions of leadership we have inherited are required of us in our present situation?* And that is a more difficult question. As we indicated at the start, there is no way that a single report from a central Commission can answer this question. What is needed instead are multiple wise experiments *in situ*, and prayerful scrutiny of the fruit of those experiments over time.

170 What we can provide in this report, instead of attempting a direct answer to these questions, is a two-fold response.

171 The first response is simply *encouragement* to diverse and creative improvisation upon our tradition, in the light of its sources. It is a tradition of experimentation in multiple contexts, and to continue it faithfully requires that we continue that experimentation in our own contexts. We should not be looking for a single template, process, strategy or formula that will tell us what to look for in prospective senior leaders, or what the roles of senior leaders should be.

172 The second is a set of *guidelines for thoughtful scrutiny* – a description of the kind of reflection we will need if our creative improvisations are to be faithful. These guidelines flow from what we have already said about leadership in the New Testament church, but there are some key points worth emphasising again.

5.1 Keeping God at the centre

173 As our triangle diagrams indicate, the triune God must remain at the centre of all our ideas and practices of leadership. We cannot hold a meaningful conversation about leadership except in the context of our understanding of the *missio Dei*, the mission of God in the world.

174 Any true leadership in the church will emerge as an aspect of the Spirit's work conforming the whole body together to Christ, in relation to the Father. Its proper discernment and development therefore requires constant, prayerful, humble and attentive listening by the whole church, and especially by those who exercise leadership within it, to what the Spirit may be saying to God's people. Wise improvisation in leadership will therefore only emerge from communities and individuals gathered by the Spirit in sustained prayer and worship, with the Son, before the Father.

175 We also need to keep our leadership language and practice under critical review – all of it, wherever it has come from, and whether it is traditional or recently borrowed or invented – as there is no quick way of confirming whether we are being faithful, either in our innovations or in our repetitions, except by careful, prayerful testing together, in openness to God's judgment.

5.2 Leading in the midst of the people

176 The first triangle that we described above – joining God, people and leaders – underlines the fact that leadership is always one ministry among others. It is one of the gifts that the Spirit gives for the building up of the whole body of Christ, and it is given for the sake of the whole ministry and mission of God's people. It is one of the ways in which God is, by the Spirit, drawing the church into Christ-like life. That is why (as we said at the beginning) we cannot hold a meaningful conversation about leadership in isolation from the urgent and necessary conversations taking place about the mission and ministry of the whole people of God. Within the church, leadership is always exercised in and for the body of Christ. To paraphrase T.W. Manson, 'Things are very far wrong when the bishop – or indeed any member of the Body of Christ – has become a cog in a machine. But while cog-in-a-machine is too low a status for any Christian, member of the Body of Christ, partaker of His Spirit, and sharer of His Ministry is not too high for any. In any case there is no other.'[71]

177 Even the ministry of oversight, of *episkope*, is first of all a ministry of all God's people, who are called to exercise self-control and hold one another to account. Some, however, are called to a special exercise of this ministry of oversight for the sake of 'building up' the wider body – some at a very local scale,

71 Manson, *The Church's Ministry*, p. 30.

others on a wider stage, and some at the 'trans-local' level that we have been exploring. In that sense, today's rediscovery of the ministry of the laity (whether experienced as charismatic renewal or simply as a pragmatic result of pastoral re-organisation) represents the re-emergence of a pattern of ministry closer to that of the New Testament. At whatever scale it operates, however, this call to *episkope* includes a call to attend to, to encourage, to guide and to work with the ministries of every member of God's people.

178 These new patterns of ministry place new demands on both clergy and laity. Clergy are much more likely now to find themselves working in a 'leadership team' or managing a confusing variety of lay ministries. They increasingly report finding their time taken up in 'management' rather than in front-line pastoral work.[72] Again, it is refreshing to return to the Pauline churches and discover that 'leadership' (whatever you call it) is just one among many of the gifts of the Spirit – but that it is a real gift, demanding specific skills and real respect (leadership as a two-way process). Paul's letters are a rich resource for practical models for teamwork and collaborative ministry, operating in a much more fluid and complex ministry structure than what we once used to regard as the 'norm' of the traditional parish.[73]

179 This also suggests that the way in which senior church leaders share ministry among themselves is of great importance. Here we touch again on some of the issues raised in Section 1, including the relationship within dioceses between diocesan and suffragan bishops, between bishops and archdeacons, and between ordained and lay leaders, and parallel sets of

---

72 This is one of the clearest findings from recent Ministry Division research exercises, and of studies such as Croft, *Ministry in Three Dimensions*, ch. 1.

73 For a refreshing and engaging dialogue between Paul's leadership style and contemporary management theory, see Richard S. Ascough and Sandy Cotton, *Passionate Visionary: Leadership Lessons from the Apostle Paul*, Peabody, MA: Hendrickson, 2006.

relationships between senior leaders within cathedrals and at national church level. In each case, there is a need to make space for careful reflection on the patterns of relationship between all those entrusted with senior leadership, and between them and those they work with and serve. Leaders in these contexts need to exercise authority, responsibility, accountability, collegiality and prayerful discernment together in a way that seeks God's kingdom above all else and reflects the underlying pattern of the self-emptying servant leadership of Christ (Philippians 2.1–11).

180 The exercise of collegial leadership needs particular reflection in the current climate of public accountability around issues such as safeguarding. Collegiality should not be confused with collusion, nor with a refusal to accept individual responsibility for standing out (where necessary) against a culture of corruption.[74] A collegial model of leadership does not mean that everyone has exactly the same responsibilities, the same tasks. Some will be individual responsibilities, and some will be common, but the individual ones will also be fulfilled in consultation with the rest of the college and in the light of common goals and concerns, not 'held' and used to hoard knowledge-as-power. This is an important aspect of leadership at diocesan level, in particular regarding issues of abuse and clergy discipline. It is important not to encourage a false dichotomy here between individual and shared leadership: what matters is doing collegial leadership properly, which means having individual tasks and responsibilities clearly framed within a context of shared working and mutual accountability.

74 A point made in the *Interim Report of the Commissaries Appointed by the Archbishop of Canterbury in Relation to a Visitation upon the Diocese of Chichester* (2012), http://safeguarding.chichester.anglican.org/documents/archbishops-visitation/archbishops-commissaries-interim-report/.

5.3 Leadership and discipleship

181 Leaders respond to their particular call alongside the calls of each of God's people, and in the context of the whole people's common call to love and serve the Lord. They are not 'above' others, even if their calling often requires them (literally and metaphorically) to stand up in front of others. Any of our language and practices that embed attitudes of superiority need to be resisted, as do ways of living that tend to separate those with leadership responsibilities from the shared experience of the 'ordinary' church.

182 Those whom God is calling in this way to lead can nevertheless have a proper ambition: an emerging personal discernment of their call, a recognition of the gifts that God has given them for it, and a growing desire to serve God's work in obedience to it. The discernment of a leader's calling is not, however, simply a personal matter. The individual leader's discernment interacts with and is tested by the discernment of the wider body – so that we could say that any proper ambition to lead will not simply be the individual leader's ambition but will be an aspiration shared with the community.

183 If our understanding of leadership has its place within our understanding of the Spirit's work, conforming the people of God to Christ, then it has its place within our understanding of sanctification – God's work in us drawing us deeper into holiness. Yet to exercise senior leadership in the life of the church makes very great demands on a person's spiritual life and can create very great obstacles to growth in love and holiness (hence the repeated advice to monks in the early centuries to avoid episcopal office at all costs). This is one reason why senior leadership in the church was traditionally linked with the ordained ministry, with its built-in commitment to a life formed by the Eucharist. The welcome opening-up of senior roles to lay people raises the question: what patterns of training and support do we need to ensure that all leaders – whether lay or ordained – are equally committed to the fundamental practices of discipleship and have the constant prayer and support of those around them?

184 Recognition of a call to lead also, therefore, means recognition of a call to share in an accompanying spiritual discipline. Leaders must, with the help of the wider community, be on their guard against the temptations associated with leadership: the temptation to isolate their own discernment from the discernment of the body, the temptation to focus on building a name or a legacy for themselves at the expense of building up the body, and the temptation to desire leadership for its own sake.

5.4 Acknowledging failure

185 As we pursue diverse improvisations in leadership, we must not mistake failure for disaster. Some improvisations will fail – or, at least, they will not produce the renewal or the growth or the depth that we hoped for. Sometimes, there may be lessons that our prayerful reflection can learn from such failures; often, even with the benefit of hindsight, it will be hard to see what else could have been done. The growth of God's kingdom is in God's hands. We must pray all we can, learn all we can and work all we can, but these are not handles that need only to be turned hard to guarantee success.

186 We therefore have to cultivate a culture that allows failure, that attends to it carefully and learns from it seriously, but that does not condemn it. In part, this is because we will certainly not encourage real improvisation and experimentation if we have generated an atmosphere of performance anxiety; improvisation is only made possible by trust. More seriously, however, it is because any understanding of Christian leadership that believes success to be firmly in the grasp of good leaders, rather than in the hands of God, has become a form of idolatry. The one true leader of the church is God, Father, Son and Holy Spirit, and true success is in God's hands alone.

5.5 Attending to the local and the trans-local

187 Our second triangle – joining God, local leaders and trans-local leaders – underlines the interdependence of the local and the trans-local. We are inheritors of a complex ongoing negotiation between local and trans-local – a shifting division of labour between the local church and wider structures of co-ordination and communication. That division of labour has shifted continually throughout Christian history, and our own experiments will go on drawing the boundary in different places and in different ways – but in all of them will need to find ways of doing justice to both the local and the trans-local: to the unity of the body of Christ, and to the embeddedness which the Spirit gives it in each and every location.

188 One thing is, however, clear: local and trans-local leadership are interdependent. What originally defined the office of the bishop was that it holds together both of these: rooted in responsibility (for life, according to the canons of Nicaea) for a specific group of Christian communities defined by place, yet also in accountability to the church of God in every place through patterns of episcopal collegiality. This mediation of the local and trans-local is an important element of what 'senior leadership' means in the Church of England.

189 It is also clear that our definitions of locality may need to change with a changing world. *Mission-Shaped Church* and the Fresh Expressions movement have challenged us to think more searchingly about what we mean by 'locality': is our 'locality' where we eat and sleep and send our children to school (and not much else), or where most adults spend their waking hours – namely, in the workplace? Is it where we shop? Or is it the virtual world we inhabit when we're on-line? What are we doing to resource a Christian presence in those (equally real) localities, and how do they relate to the actual physical church buildings that imprint God's presence so powerfully on our landscape?[75]

5.6 Identifying the tasks of leadership

190 Any attempts we make to identify the specific tasks of senior leaders must flow primarily from our understanding of the ministry and mission for which God has called the church into being by Word and Spirit, rather than from some generic account of organisational leadership.

191 In the specific case of bishops, although the precise arrangements and forms have changed constantly, there have been strong strands of continuity woven through those changes. We began by looking to Canon C 18 and the Ordinal for an expression of this: the bishop is chief pastor; called to teach and to admonish; called to be an example of righteous and godly living; called to oversight of sacramental ministry; and called to recognise and commission others in the church for their own forms of public ministry (see above, §43). In a rather different idiom, we might refer instead to the main headings from our exploration of the New Testament: the ministry and mission that the bishop serves are matters of word, worship, work and world – that is, of preaching, teaching and admonition; of prayer and sacramental ministry; of caring labour for the welfare of the people; and of networking around the wider church and representation of the church in public. These tasks have remained constant through the long history of the church, though their distribution between different parts of the structure (local and trans-local, lay and ordained) has changed over time. The important thing is that the church as a whole remains faithful to her calling.

---

75 *Fresh Expressions in the Mission of the Church*, ch. 5.

192 A healthy account of senior leadership in the church will keep these matters at its heart: they are the forms of leadership specific to the church and its collective task of ministry and mission. Other, more generic tasks of leadership and management may well be necessary to allow the whole collective practice to function well, and they may at times be of very great importance, but those further tasks should always be oriented toward the practice of ministry and mission, and we should take care not to let them become ends in themselves. Management in the church exists only for the sake of ministry and mission, and it must not get in their way. This is precisely why it is crucial to understand leadership as a form of 'stewardship', equipping and resourcing the saints for their work of ministry in the world. As stewards, leaders are called to faithfulness (1 Corinthians 4.1): they are custodians, not owners, and have no authority to change the ultimate goal of the whole enterprise – though it may be their task to reflect on proximate objectives as means to attain the desired end. Leadership is always subservient to the goals and ethos of the whole body.

5.7 Attending to the context

193 Successful improvisation will also require sustained attention to the contexts in which the church finds itself. Overviews and generalisations, and reports on what experiments have worked in other contexts, are important ingredients in our improvisations – important sources of inspiration, guidance and caution – but they are not the whole recipe.

194 We also need sustained prayerful attention to the social locations, the cultures and the histories of the places in which the church finds itself; sustained prayerful attention to the composition and character of the local churches; sustained prayerful attention to the different strengths and experiences that individual leaders bring with them, often including their experience of service in a variety of 'secular' worlds.

195 We should be very wary indeed of approaches to the development of leadership that push towards uniformity, not least because they tend to mistake models grown in very particular soil (a compost of hidden assumptions about gender, class, race and culture) for universal schemes. The hallmark of the Spirit's work is variety – a diversified Christlikeness, never twice the same.

5.8 Improvising within a tradition

196 Successful musical improvisation depends on a deep training in the musical tradition – an intimate knowledge of the possibilities of scales and harmonies, of rhythms and melodies. In the same way, faithful improvisation in leadership requires communities and individuals deeply grounded in the Christian faith, knowing it well enough and richly enough to be able to see new ways of living it out appropriate to the new contexts in which they find themselves.

197 Tradition and innovation are not opposed, because deep immersion in tradition is not an awkward constraint upon improvisation but is its enabling condition. The more improvisation we want, the deeper the forms of education we will need – and the deeper those forms of education will need to take us into knowledge of the tradition and knowledge of the Scriptures. The need for ongoing education that takes them ever deeper into the Scriptures' witness to Christ, and the changing patterns of the church's response to that witness, is as urgent for senior leaders as it is for any other member of the body – and the need for such ongoing education needs to be a prominent part of our thinking about the selection and support of senior leaders, lay and ordained.

198 Above all, faithful improvisation will only emerge from communities and individuals who are brought by the Spirit, in the company of all the saints, to deeper and deeper knowledge of Christ, and him crucified.

Some questions for further study

As a 'resource for reflection', this report is not intended to produce a set of straightforward practical recommendations for the practice of senior leadership in the Church of England. Our exploration of the nature of leadership does, however, yield a set of questions that it is appropriate to pose to our practices of senior leadership, at national and diocesan level, as well as in other contexts.

- How do we identify those being called to senior leadership, and what are the processes of prayerful corporate discernment by which those identifications are tested? How are those processes rooted in our wider practices of discerning the gifts and callings of every member of God's people?
- In what ways are we providing for and supporting ongoing discernment, capable of identifying necessary changes to roles, relationships and tasks?
- Are our processes of identification and discernment producing the leaders we need to serve the ministry and mission of the church in the world? Are they fostering faithful improvisation? Are we fostering a culture of leadership that allows failure?
- How do we ensure that, with all the demands of management, senior leaders can focus on their vocation to lead people deeper into ministry and mission as disciples of Christ?
- Does the collegiality between different kinds of senior leader in a given context (for example, a diocese) help to make this focus on the gospel possible, by allowing a division of labour? Is it structured in such a way that the various leaders involved can hold one another to account in the light of this primary vocation? How can we deepen the ecology of relationships among senior leaders in this context?

- How are we ensuring that senior leaders are closely engaged with the people they serve – closely enough to be challenged by them and learn from them?
- In what ways are senior leaders enabled to learn the particularities of their contexts together, and how is that knowledge passed on, tested and enriched?
- In what ways are we providing for and supporting senior leaders' ongoing learning, including their ongoing engagement together with Scripture and tradition? Are we creating a learning culture, within which the learning of the whole people of God, and within that the learning required of leaders, can flourish together?
- In what ways are we making space for and supporting the spiritual disciplines vital to senior leadership? Do any of our structures or processes unnecessarily work against those disciplines? Do we give senior leaders the space, the tools and the support they need for self-reflection, including honest and searching self-criticism?

Senior leadership in the church is one of the many gifts that God gives to animate and shape its ministry and mission. It is a gift to the body of Christ, locally and trans-locally; it is discerned by the body, and exercised in, with and for the body; it helps to build up and guide the body in its task of witness. But it is given to the body only so that Christ may be more luminously visible in its life and audible in its speech, so that the world might believe. The deepest question that we can ask, and must go on asking, of all our arrangements for senior leadership is: Do they serve this task?

Appendix: Synod reports relating to episcopacy

Bishops and Dioceses (Advisory Council for the Church's Ministry), the report of the Ministry Committee Working Party on the Episcopate. GS 63 (1971).

Episcopacy in the Church of England, a consultative document by Paul A. Welsby. GS 167 (1973).

The Theology of Ordination, a report by the Faith and Order Advisory Group of The Board for Mission and Unity. GS 281 (1976).

Episcopacy and the Role of the Suffragan Bishops, a report by the Dioceses Commission. GS 551 (1982).

The Priesthood of the Ordained Ministry, General Synod Board for Mission and Unity. GS 694 (1986).

Episcopal Ministry, the report of the Archbishops' Group on the Episcopate, sometimes referred to as 'The Cameron Report'. GS 944 (1990).

Senior Church Appointments: A Review of the Methods of Appointment of Area and Suffragan Bishops, Deans, Provosts, Archdeacons and Residentiary Canons, the report of a working party established by the Standing Committee of the Church of England. GS 1019 (1993).

Working with the Spirit: Choosing Diocesan Bishops. A Review of the Crown Appointments Commission and Related Matters. GS 1405 (2001). https://www.churchofengland.org/media/1268522/gs1405.pdf

Suffragan Bishops, House of Bishops Occasional Paper. GS Misc 733 (2004). https://www.churchofengland.org/media/40660/gsmisc733suffbps.doc

Women Bishops in the Church of England?, a report of the House of Bishops' Working Party on Women in the Episcopate, sometimes referred to as 'The Rochester Report'. GS 1557 (2004). https://www.churchofengland.org/media/1258758/gs1557.pdf

Part 2

Sources for Theological Reflection on Leadership

2.1 Leadership and Ministry in the sub- and post-Apostolic Period

Cally Hammond

> When someone said to Leonidas, son of Anaxandridas, brother of Cleomenes, "If you were not king you would be no different from us", Leonidas replied, "But if I were not better than you, I would not be king."[1]

Why might ancient and modern models of senior leadership seem to be pulling in different directions? This paper surveys the portrayal of character and leadership in patristic Christian and other ancient texts, looking for insights into how those cultures define and image their leaders to express what they need from them. It then suggests what today's Church can learn from the comparison.

It may be that current preoccupation with the theory and practice of leadership is generated by the anxiety about direction and purpose in the Church in the twenty-first century that emerges in a hierarchically stratified institution embedded in a theoretically egalitarian society. Looking at how leadership worked in the early centuries of Christianity will cast light on that current situation. Then, hierarchy was a social 'given', and questioning of the need for leaders and leadership did not arise. Now, hierarchy is still present in reality, but is masked by theoretical principles (and the accompanying rhetoric) of equality. As a result, leadership has

1 Plutarch, *Apophthegmata Laconica* 1.

continually to be justified by recourse to arguments not based on the old qualifying criteria of birth, wealth, territorial influence, and social connections, and so is more heavily reliant upon criteria such as achievements and experience. In those early centuries, though, it is also true that the Church had the capacity to be socially radical, given that her leadership was based not only on the traditional factors mentioned earlier (birth, wealth, territorial influence, social connections) but also upon an alternative set of criteria centred on *charism*. Other religions in the ancient Mediterranean, including Judaism, with a self-identity tied to factors of place and blood, developed leadership systems based on traditional factors like ancestral descent, benefaction or wealth. Christianity cast its leadership net wider than this, and it is tempting to suppose that recognising and 'promoting' the talented in addition to the well-born was a significant factor in the successful spread of the faith.

If leaders possess none of the talents necessary to move and motivate others, and to effect change, they are not tolerated for long in either the ancient or the modern world. The ancient world was, of course, very limited in terms of modes of communication for exercising such control; but prominent in the educational curriculum was rhetoric, which can be defined as the techniques, skills and theory of the art of persuasive speech. Senior leaders in the early Church, as well as in 'pagan' society, depended heavily on rhetorical abilities in the conduct of their public role.[2] They learned how to present themselves, how to construct arguments, how to put words together for maximum emotional and intellectual effect, both in order to engage with the world of non-Christians all around them, and to exercise influence within the Christian community. They were well prepared for countering (in speech or writing) the attacks of non-Christians on the intelligibility of Christianity. Such leaders were

---

2 This remained true until the fifth century. Cyril's arguments against Nestorius show no evidence of education in Classical rhetoric (though many of the argumentative techniques remained embedded, of course). Ancient rhetoric in patristic texts both compels and repels the modern reader with its combination of invective and repetition, a sign that the texts are written to be heard, as much as read.

expected to be men of intellectual, moral and spiritual stature. What is less clearly understood is that for these qualities to be evident they needed to be *communicators* who were also *persuaders*: in other words, experts in rhetoric.

Studying Leadership in the Early Church

When we consider 'leadership' in the early Church, we must always bear in mind that our source materials are fragmentary, biased and interpolated. They do not give a complete or balanced picture of the early Church in its administration or 'mission', or in its leadership. They incline towards an agenda that is pushing strongly for the exclusion of variety and diversity first in ideology (often referred to as dogma, doctrine, or theology) and then in praxis (the actions which both encode and shape such ideologies: sacraments, rituals, and the social outworkings of religious group identity).

It is also important that episcopacy, episcopal authority, and the hierarchical power structure of holy orders, should not be analysed as if they were somehow destined or fated to develop in such a manner, and to such a conclusion. The emergence of the threefold order of bishops, priests and deacons took a long time, and searching for how it happened can tempt scholars to play down or dismiss the diversity of ministries evident in early Christianity. In this period, it was a given that a truly apostolic Christian community could not act or think as if past history were 'wrong'. The tendency for post-Nicene Church Councils to look back to Nicaea as a 'gold standard' of authority and orthodoxy became stronger as time passed. Christian ideology inclined towards interpreting change in terms of development, rather than alteration, of tradition; the drive to isolate and impose uniformity was very strong.

The bias of sources referred to above directs us to look at male ordained leadership in the public sphere as the primary model or 'type', rather than focusing on – say – the inculcation of Christian values in the domestic sphere, which may have been a principally female role, as famously in the case of Augustine and his mother Monnica. If we express an implied acceptance of that bias by merely glancing at other forms of leadership before moving on to the 'leadership which matters', what we are really saying is that the question currently at issue is not about leadership per se but leadership in the public sphere. This is a clearer category than 'senior', because it potentially includes both young people and leaders whose leadership does not entail high status, though the term 'senior' does imply that criteria such as age (with concomitant experience) are being prioritised.

The *Paterfamilias* as Leader

The emergence of episcopacy has been minutely investigated by scholars and need not be repeated here.[3] It is nonetheless important to consider whether the development of models of Church leadership in a family (or better 'household' or 'domestic') context has consequences for how Church leadership subsequently operates, and how it is understood and consented to by the main body of believers. In the Roman Empire, leadership within the family was exercised by a *paterfamilias*, an adult male who had legal responsibility for all those within his household (including slaves); the duties and rights of a *paterfamilias* gave him *de facto* as well as *de iure* authority. The language of consanguinity and familial ties (parent/child, husband/wife, brothers/sisters) could also, within early Christian ideology, be applied to the relationship between the Christian group/individual and God. Understanding leadership in terms of parenthood could therefore be exceptionally powerful, relating the earthly leader to (usually) his divine counterpart.

---

3 E.g. James A. Mohler, *The Origin and Evolution of the Priesthood*, Staten Island, NY: Alba, 1969; Edward Schillebeeckx, *Ministry: Leadership in the Community of Jesus Christ*, New York, NY: Crossroad, 1981; Allen Brent, *The Imperial Cult and the Development of Church Order: Concepts and Images of Authority in Paganism and Early Christianity before the age of Cyprian*, Leiden: Brill, 1999; Francis A. Sullivan, *From Apostles to Bishops: The Development of the Episcopacy in the Early Church*, New York, NY: Newman, 2001.

In time, there developed orders of ministry tied to particular sacramental functions; here too this familial model of authority would have been relevant, for a *paterfamilias* also had a religious role within the domestic sphere. Not all the criteria of fitness for leadership would be comprehensible today: moral and sacral 'fitness' in the early Church did not embrace a principle of equality of all humankind, whether able-bodied or with disabilities, male or female, ethnic minority, slave or free. Conformity to a physical norm was commonly accepted as a reasonable requirement for performing sacral religious functions. The canons of Nicaea, for example, in AD 325 were emphatic in laying down physical, as well as moral and spiritual, standards for those in holy orders: if they had been forcibly castrated for example, they could continue in the clergy, but if they had mutilated themselves willingly, they must cease to act as clergy (this is laid down in canon 1 – and the placing of this says something about their understanding of priorities for leaders). They also embraced a range of hierarchical principles: no bishop, priest or deacon might live with any unrelated women (canon 3), or lend money at interest (canon 17); a bishop must be constituted by all the other bishops of his province, or, if need be, by at least three (canon 4). The threefold order was to be observed, according to Nicaea, in strictly hierarchical terms: the most sacred functions were reserved to the bishops, the lesser to the priests, the least to the deacons (canon 18). Deaconesses were to be counted as laity because they did not receive imposition of hands (canon 19). This is strict hierarchy designed for demarcation purposes: the requirements for senior leadership embrace physical, moral, sacramental and social factors.

Bishops and the Identity of the Church

The reason why bishops are central to the 'senior leadership' question is, in theory, because the term 'bishop' (*episkopos*) starts off in the NT as a term for what certain leaders did, what function(s) they exercised, rather than the title of a role to which they were appointed. In those early centuries senior Christian leaders might be chosen on criteria mainly of ability, or mainly of status, but the power of family as a 'type' of the Church both in its coherence (unity in multiplicity) and in its hierarchical relationships was further underlined by the iconic significance of the *continuity of the episcopal succession* as a guarantor of identity and teaching among Christians. It has a parallel function to consanguinity (a vital factor in Roman civic life) in forming the basis of a self-replicating social group – indispensable when racial and cultural identity do not define the group in a way which can be transmitted down the generations. Senior leaders were, and are, a primary public face of the institution that is the Church: they were, and are, treated as symbols of what the institution really *is*. From early times they have formed the interface between the institution and what exists outside itself.

The reason why leadership in the early Church still matters today is because as a social group the Church persists through time only by the exercise of mechanisms for transmitting her self-identifying features from one generation to the next. Such mechanisms included then (and still include) sacramental practices such as baptism and the eucharist; intellectual ones such as the study of sacred texts; liturgical ones such as participation in common worship; and spiritual ones such as immersion in the common deposit of faith, the 'rule of truth'[4] or 'whole package' of Christianity. This is a major reason for exploring senior leadership – the Church needs the right people to bring about that same goal of transmitting the 'whole package,' undistorted and complete, into the future.

Early Christianity, then, is defined more by ideology and liturgical praxis than by nationality or geography (though in later centuries this picture changes considerably). This makes necessary senior leaders who are *teachers*, versed in the sacred texts, competent to communicate the ideology, the beliefs and common stories; and also *priests* (for want of a better single term), able to express those

4 See Irenaeus, *Against Heresies* 1.2.1 etc.; later also referred to as 'rule of faith'.

beliefs and ideas in terms of corporate religious praxis, and the proper modelling of ritual actions. The existence of such leaders, therefore, is by definition a focus for unity because without them to embody the coherence of the 'whole package' of faith, the 'rule of truth', Christianity cannot be transmitted from one generation to the next with any certainty that it is authentic, faithful to its roots and core identity. Continuity with the 'original' 'apostolic' teaching and model of leadership remains an essential part of how the Church identifies itself into the present day.

There are two basic models for the emergence of the 'whole package' of faith. Either it was an original deposit of faith attacked by corruptions and perversions, but defended and preserved untainted; or it was a core complex of elements which developed gradually through time via a process of trial and rejection of anything inconsistent or incoherent. The latter model is more historically plausible, and more constructive for using early Christianity's experiences to reflect upon the twenty-first century Church. The power of the Christian message demands a clear expression of identity, based on key beliefs and behaviours. When different early Christian groups drew the line between the 'core' and the 'periphery' in different places, so giving no single united front on theological and ethical questions, their leaders used their status and abilities to promote the version of the core to which they themselves inclined. The 'deposit of faith' model was, and is, often preferred by leaders because of its clarity and relative simplicity; leaders who argue for the 'core complex' model will always have a harder case to make, particularly so when the hierarchical model of leadership ('Father knows best') has been displaced by a more meritocratic model. This is because estimations of the leader's merit may depend upon the version of the 'rule of truth' or 'whole package' of Christian faith that they espouse. So it is that family or tribal or group loyalty can still play as big a part in disagreements in the twenty-first century Church as does theology, and bishops draw their congregations in different directions according to their own convictions and priorities.

So the Church faces a theological conundrum when change is required. It cannot be presented as a departure from, but only a development of, precedent. Once the leadership of the Church had been reduced, over centuries, to include only adult males without physical defect and of a particular moral, intellectual and spiritual status, it became harder to develop theological justifications for reopening the criteria for access to leadership positions (as, for example, the Church of England has recently done). One early example of this emerged in the fourth century, as the Church became embedded in the life of the Empire and bishops began to accrue social and legal as well as religious authority. At the same time, a different kind of leadership was coming to prominence: the increasing prestige associated with asceticism privileged those who had proven their worth by undergoing physical privations either willingly as monastics or forcibly as confessors. It was a form of leadership outside the boundaries of official Church control: and was correspondingly open to suspicion that such leaders were building power bases, or misusing their influence.

Women and Leadership

In this period there was no place for women in the Church's ordained leadership, but another way was emerging in which they could exercise authority, one influenced by the monastic movement. The 'goddesses, wives, whores and slaves' list,[5] which encapsulated every way of being a woman in the pre-Christian Classical world, had now to incorporate another female 'type', the consecrated virgin, who (not least on the analogy of the Vestals of 'pagan' Rome) carried considerable moral and spiritual authority by reason of her 'purity'. Such women, untainted by the infection of sexual activity which rendered other women polluted and inferior, or which burdened

5 Sarah Pomeroy, *Goddesses, Wives, Whores and Slaves: Women in Classical Antiquity*, New York, NY: Schoken, 1975.

them with childbearing,[6] could, and did, intervene in public affairs and exercise influence there. Not that married women were entirely excluded from roles of power and authority, but they did need a high degree of wealth in order to devolve their traditional responsibilities onto others.[7] Helena, Eudoxia, Justina, Theodora: they all exercised forms of leadership, much as, say, Cornelia (mother of the Gracchi) and Livia (wife of Augustus) had done in the Republican and early imperial periods.[8] But they are not easily incorporated into our developing model of 'leadership in the early Church' because their authority derived from their selves, the combining of a personality and character with a role and situation, without any support from the traditional, male sources of leadership legitimation (army, priesthood, legislature), or by birthright. They were subject to judgment and criticism of their actions, which were evaluated in moral terms rather than interpreted in psychological terms by historians at the time.[9] But the same basic division operated in the case of the male leaders also: ancient commentators evaluated them morally on the basis of an assessment of their actions and achievements, which depended on pre-formed ideas of what is 'good,' 'just', or 'desirable' – and that nexus of pre-formed ideas has deep roots in the foundation myths and narratives of their cultural milieu.

---

6 Marina Warner, *Alone of All Her Sex: The Myth and Cult of the Virgin Mary*, 2nd edn, London: Pan, 1985, esp. pp. 50–67.

7 A situation which persists into the present era.

8 Mother of the emperor Constantine; wife of the emperor Arcadius and enemy of John Chrysostom; wife of the emperor Valentinian I, regent for Valentinian II, and Arian opponent of Ambrose; wife of the emperor Justinian.

9 For this fundamental distinction see Christopher Gill, 'The character-personality distinction' in Christopher Pelling (ed.), *Characterization and Individuality in Greek Literature*, Oxford: Clarendon, 1990, pp. 1–31; also Jo-Ann A. Brant, Charles W. Hedrick and Chris Shea (eds), *Ancient Fiction: The Matrix of Early Christian And Jewish Narrative*, Atlanta, GA: SBL, 2005. On the dangers of solipsistic leadership see Achilles in the *Iliad*; or Coriolanus in early Roman historiography. Strong leadership is not always successful, or cohesive: see Tim Cornell, 'Coriolanus: Myth, History and Performance' in David Braund and Christopher Gill (eds), *Myth, History And Culture In Republican Rome: Studies in Honour of T.P. Wiseman*, Exeter: University of Exeter Press, 2003, pp. 73–97.

Contrasting Models for Leadership

Where are the good models for leaders? The Old Testament is full of leaders both male and female, but evaluation of their 'goodness' is problematised by the clashes of values inevitable over such long phases of history within the Old Testament taken as a whole. The New Testament, on the other hand, is dogged by the problem that despite examples of typically 'good' leaders such as Paul and Peter (both of them fine examples for persuasive speech, one of the most valuable assets of the leader, as evidenced both by biblical and patristic texts), the supreme example (Jesus) re-wrote the 'type' by becoming passive rather than active, pacific rather than assertive, silent rather than eloquent, deserted rather than supported (support from the multitude is always an important criterion of leadership skill in ancient narrative), and killed rather than surviving. There are strands in the gospels supporting both the familiar active-leader 'type' and this strange new passive 'type';[10] they are imperfectly integrated, but in the combining of them subsists the possibility of widening the scope of our understanding of leadership in the Church today.

Charisma and Rhetoric

To clarify further the nature of 'leadership' it is helpful to ask what may be the organs of change in society: in the ancient world these could include the family or kinship group or tribe; the army; the legislature (monarchic, oligarchic, democratic); the legal system; the sacral system (priests, embeddedness of religion in public life); and the intellectual milieu where new understandings and ideas were explored between people of influence and ability. Christianity added another, quite new, kind of authority-source: the holy books,

10 Roman historiography also contains examples of leaders whose 'failures' (by the norms of moral assessment of action) are repackaged as 'successes' – Coriolanus, Fabius Cunctator, Cicero etc.

τὰ βιβλία, and specialists to interpret them (commentators like Origen; theorists like Augustine). Leadership needed to co-operate with these sources of authority, otherwise it could appear dangerous, subversive, and deserving of moral condemnation. In addition to the question of organs and structures, there were personal qualities and skills which leaders needed to lay claim to. It is part of the deep mythology of early Christianity that those who 'led' the Way in its beginning were simple and unlettered, without advantages of rank or inculcated eloquence. When the New Testament text then revealed them to be both eloquent in their speech and powerful in their effects, the credit went to the energising, transforming power of the Holy Spirit. Whatever the source of such eloquence, the combination of persuasive speech (the bedrock of a Classical education) and personal charisma was as effective in early Christian history as it was in the narratives of the pre-Christian period at exercising leadership and effecting change. Whether those two factors can be taught or not is another matter. Just as now, teaching was then a trade – teachers needed paying pupils to make a living. Persuasive speech was not a skill all could master, any more than all could acquire a charismatic personality. But those who absorbed the lessons of rhetoric at the highest level would have acquired a unique tool – or weapon. It could be modulated to suit any situation. In this was real power – the capacity to exercise influence, and to effect change. The person who could speak persuasively could control the legislature, the judiciary, the army, the intelligentsia; or the Church.

Limits to the Study of Ancient Leadership

It could be argued that to understand leadership in the early Church all we need to do is read the documents and locate examples. If we proceed thus, the documents will yield military leaders like Constantine and Justinian; bishops who were also politicians like Ambrose, John Chrysostom and Athanasius; bishops who were theologians before all else, like Augustine and Gregory of Nyssa.

They will tend to privilege those who fit the ancient 'type' of a leader in terms of birth and background, education, and character. Those, on the other hand, who cross boundaries or who are in some way 'interstitial' are judged negatively. Arius, for example, was damned, by the time his story was written up, by a century of vilification; Nestorius was criticised for pugnacious dogmatism, Julian for folly and incompetence, and Hypatia for presumption (according to one account) and witchcraft (according to another). The same documents endorse the kinds of leader that our cultural mythology and history also incline us to prefer: action heroes, people of stature and ability, of moral courage or sharp intellect. And they shape the complex, messy reality of individual leaders' actions into simple, familiar moral types, to ease the process of interpretation and prioritisation.[11]

Those documents will not yield us a picture of how leadership functioned at every level of the Church's life. It is difficult to reconstruct catechetical practice, or the education of Christian children within the family. It is also difficult to reconstruct Church life at the everyday level of co-existence in a multicultural environment – the best evidence for this is probably sermons, which give us the reactions of disappointed preachers to their unappreciative or disobedient flocks. If we ask ourselves, 'What were the *episkopoi* overseeing?' the answer comes back that they were leaders of a socially diverse, ideologically united group or groups we call the early Church, whose strength, effectiveness, and growth was rooted in the power of her core message, which in turn depended for its dissemination upon the development of a cohesive leadership structure and/or hierarchy of leadership within early Christian communities.

---

11 Christopher Pelling, *Literary Texts and the Greek Historian*, London: Routledge, 2000, p. 6, 'Juries are readier to believe stories which fit patterns familiar from fiction, normally ... television.'

Leadership and Unity

In the understanding of early Church leadership, some polarities are fundamental: just as there was a contrast (mentioned above) between bishops as establishment figures of authority and monastic leaders whose charismatic authority was not moderated by any establishment, so also there was a contrast between sacred ministers as representing their congregation to God (collegial bishops/presbyters) and sacred ministers as representing God to their congregation (*monepiscope*). The patristic witness was emphatic about leadership, whether conciliar or monarchical, established or charismatic, not being a matter of birth or age, but of gift. The Holy Spirit must be discerned; there must be indisputable evidence of sound apostolic truth in that person's teaching; their charism would entitle them to the respect and obedience of the people and clergy, who were not to dispute with, or separate themselves from, their bishop. Marcion is a clear example of one who so separated himself – and whose ideas, because he was both schismatic and heretical, dwindled away into oblivion. The early Church could endure a degree of schism (practical diversity) but not of heresy (ideological diversity); it could be argued that the Church today is in the opposite position, and that the role of senior leaders currently carries a heavier load of expectation with respect to behaving in unified ways than it does to holding unified beliefs.

Character and Personality

When the Church was a small group at odds with the prevailing culture, it needed strong leadership and cohesive teaching to survive, replicate, and expand. The Church's incorporation into the workings of Roman society in the fourth century has been identified by many as a moment of crisis in her spiritual leadership: as if by taking on the status and privileges of 'pagan' religious officials, bishops began a long, ongoing process of collusion with, instead of challenge to, the secular world. This view is both out-dated and over-simplistic.

But it does point to a divide between modern and ancient models of leadership. On the one hand there is the *action-based* type of evaluation (character); on the other, an *intention/motivation-based* one (personality). This posits an opposition between 'character,' understood as something (a) fixed and (b) apparent in a person's actions; and 'personality,' a model based on psychology and human individual uniqueness, not eternal norms. On the 'character' model, identifying and appointing 'good' people for senior appointments of any kind is relatively easy: with the eye of hindsight, those who 'reached the top' must 'deserve' to have done so. Using a more modern 'personality' model, identifying 'good' leaders is much more difficult. 'Good' has no absolute content: a good person could be a poor leader; a good leader of one group could be a poor leader of another. In this case, the qualities identified as desirable in a leader have to be related to their performance-context (as it were).

The textual witnesses of early Christianity were all generated in an era when the fixed-character model dominated, not the flexible-personality model; so it is hardly surprising if modern criteria for leadership do not map cleanly onto ancient. Once again, hierarchy is at the heart of the problem: leadership theory is plagued by the disjuncture between a hierarchically ordered institution operating within a theoretically egalitarian society. Senior leadership as an 'issue' for the Church results in part from the clash of a hierarchical leadership model with a non-hierarchical social ideology. We should not assume that the present non-hierarchical model will last for ever, or that its reality and its theory match. In effect, human beings create hierarchies in their social differentiation even when the official ideology of society prohibits or penalises this. The lesson of the patristic Church is not one of an initial 'radical democracy' model of leadership gradually infected by the evil of hierarchical Roman imperial ideology. The Church was from the beginning hierarchical, and fitted, as such, into a hierarchical milieu. Its hierarchy, however, consisted at first in the privileging of social criteria such as charism, or spiritual gifts, which slowly evolved to cohere with old categories of leadership (family, status, wealth, education).

Leadership and Persuasion

It is a 'true saying, and worthy of all men to be received' that throughout the patristic period, as well as later in Christian history, different Christian groups and individuals have held theological views which are, on occasion, incompatible. Back in the third century, Origen dared to tackle this unpalatable fact, remarking that: 'the only truth which we must believe is that which does not differ in any respect from the tradition of the Church and the apostles'[12]. Those first leaders of the Church, the apostles and their appointed successors, constituted within themselves a primary authority for what counted as authentic; and this, combined with the principle of episcopal continuity, further underlines how and why senior leadership is such a sensitive subject – the very essence of the faith may be at stake. In a context where apologetics, the defence of the reasonableness of Christianity, and its claims to be an authentic religion, were a priority, the Church's senior (in the sense of publicly recognised) leaders were absolutely essential to the conception of Church for which Origen argued. He drew attention specifically to the words of Titus 1.9, that as well as being thoroughly immersed in Scripture, good teachers, and persons of moral stature, bishops should be also competent to refute opponents. The latter required of them skill in rhetoric, the art and techniques of persuasive speech. There might be no doubt where the credit for such talents lay – with God rather than with mortals. But one of the marks of God's approval of a leader was that leader's capacity to govern people through the whole panoply of rhetorical tools and techniques.

The reason why Origen provides such an interesting test-case for the question of senior leadership in early Christianity is that he embodied a divide between the faith as a diverse movement and as a uniform one. He was distinctively individualistic in his engagements

12 Preface to *On First Principles*, §2.

with, and attitude to, authority, and after his death was condemned for not having anticipated the standards of orthodoxy in the centuries which followed his own. He was also acutely aware of the difference between theory and practice when it came to the intellectual and spiritual standards expected of bishops, and was not afraid to voice his criticisms. So his approach has been described as 'radically subversive of institutional stability.'[13] This evokes the principle that it is not the existence of intellectual and spiritual excellence in all senior Church leaders as individuals that matters, so much as the fact that such qualities are convincingly attributed to them, and that on the basis of this attribution they can govern the Church as an institution with co-operation and trust from the governed. To understand senior leadership in the early Church properly, we have to recognise that this disjuncture between attributed capacity and actual talent is one front on which the perpetual Christian battle between purism and practicality is played out. Every individual leader does not need to be perfect (indeed cannot be so): it is enough that as a group they can win the consent of those whom they lead to their having sufficient of the necessary talents and capacities, and a convincingly grounded authority. Institutional stability cannot be an end in itself but it is still indispensable if Christian leaders are to do their job in securing the transmission of the faith to generations yet to come.

> Here is no popular acclamation, no thought given to consanguinity or kinship ... the government of the people is given over to him whom God has chosen ... who has the Spirit of God.[14]

---

13 Joseph W. Trigg, 'The Charismatic Intellectual: Origen's Understanding of Religious Leadership,' *Church History* 50 (1981), pp. 5–19: p. 18.

14 Origen, *Homily on Numbers 22.4*

2.2 Considerations of Leadership in the Light of the *Rule of Benedict*

Fr Thomas Seville CR

It may seem a strange course, to look to a text written for monks 15 centuries ago[1] for something to say about leadership, in a church which has only passing acquaintance with either the Rule or its embodiment in community – even more so given that several centuries ago this church suppressed with great brutality the kind of life for which the text was written. However, in recent years there has been a recognition of the influence of Benedict on the Church of England and, although it is easy to see that this may be exaggerated, enough is present for Benedictinism to be seen as a tradition which is close to much in Anglican piety and life and which can remain a source of critical renewal and inspiration.[2]

I wish to look at the way the authority of the abbot is configured in the Rule, in a way that identifies a place of great authority but also relativises it. I will show that, in this context, 'leadership' (if it is indeed possible to apply that concept here at all) is something fundamentally de-centred, and that this is for reasons that are not peculiar to the monastic life, but apply to the church as a whole.

---

1 *The Rule of St. Benedict in Latin and English*, ed. Timothy Fry OSB, Collegeville, MN: The Liturgical Press, 1981.

2 Martin Thornton, *English Spirituality*, London: SPCK, 1962; Robert Hale, *Canterbury and Rome – Sister Churches: A Roman Catholic Monk Reflects upon Reunion in Diversity*, London: DLT, 1982; Rowan Williams, 'Benedict and the Future of Europe', Speech at St Anselmo in Rome, Tuesday 21 November 2006; available online at http://rowanwilliams.archbishopofcanterbury.org/articles.php/1770/.

The Nature of the Rule

The Rule of Benedict is a rule for monks. It is less a series of directions on how to be a monk, more a depository of practical, scripturally inspired wisdom for the life of a monastery. It is an abbreviated and significantly reworked version of an earlier text, the Rule of the Master,[3] and for its omissions and additions depends on the traditions represented by other rules and directions, such as the Rules of Augustine and of Pachomius, and the works of Cassian and Basil. Commonly attributed to Benedict, it is also the work of several redactors. It does not dictate all uses and practices in a monastery but was the point of orientation under the gospel for the community's life. Parts of it find little application now, such as the sections concerning punishment or the practical directions concerning clothes. Given by Pope Gregory to Augustine of Canterbury before his mission to England and made the normative rule in the west at Aachen in 813 by Charlemagne, it became the decisive rule for monks in the Western church and certainly has had the widest influence of any rule beyond the cenobitic (that is, communal monastic) world.

Abbots among the Baptised[4]

From the prologue to the Rule (esp. §§1–7), it is clear that the basis for the community under the Rule is the reality of baptism. Those who make up the community do so on the basis of the baptismal faith. The first word of the Rule is the command to listen, just as the one seeking baptism in the church had first to hear the word; then there is the command to repent, and then to renounce.[5] 'The focus

3 *The Rule of the Master*, tr. Luke Eberle and Charles Philippi, Kalamazoo, MI: Cistercian Publications, 1977.

4 Eoin de Bhaldraithe OCist, 'Holy Communion in the Rule of Benedict' in H. Gehrke (ed.), *Wandel und Bestand: Festschrift B. Jaspert*, Paderborn: Bonifatius, 1995, pp. 237–49.

5 Michaela Puzicha OSB, *Kommentar zur Benediktusregel*, St. Ottilien: Eos, 2002, p. 48–52.

falls on the introduction to a personal relationship to Jesus Christ and to a definite orientation to the coming kingdom of God.'[6] There is a consequent paring down of status of social gradation and minimal attention to the significance of rank. Saving the officers of the community and the abbot, the only gradation that matters is that of the date of entry.

Within this community, the office of an abbot is not institutional in the strict sense and it is not hierarchical or sacramental; it derives from the baptismal priesthood, a community of the baptised who have elected one of their number to be 'a center of unity and a guide in its search for and accomplishment of the will of God.'[7] That said, it does have features of an office which is instituted; it is not simply charismatic. It depends on the gifts of the spirit which are given to the person who has the office and to the community in which it exists. There is often a correlation between bad abbots and bad communities, good communities and good abbots.[8]

Although in the Rule an abbot is ordained, the installation is not analogous to the ordination of a cleric.[9] Indeed the office is, canonical practices notwithstanding, basically a lay office. That such a person, a layman, enjoyed a vicarious and public relation to Christ, shepherded, directed and taught communities, and was open to a charism of the Spirit, was generally accepted in the early church and not seriously contested before the ninth century.[10]

---

6 Athanasius Polag OSB, 'The Benedictine Tradition', *CR Quarterly Review* 442 (2013), pp. 1–15: p. 11.

7 Armand Veilleux, 'The Abbatial Office in Cenobitic Life', *Monastic Studies* 5 (1968), pp. 3–46, p. 39.

8 Michael Casey OCSO and David Tomlins, *Introducing Benedict's Rule: A Program of Formation*, St. Ottilien: Eos, 2006, p. 53.

9 Veilleux, 'Abbatial Office', p. 36–9; Jean-Marie Tillard O.P., 'Authority and Religious Life', *Review for Religious* 27 (1968), pp. 80–103.

10 Adalbert de Vogüé, *Community and Abbot in the Rule of Saint Benedict*, vol. 1, Kalamazoo, MI: Cistercian Studies, 1978, p. 109. Though not allowed at present in the Roman Catholic church, it is permitted in some Anglican communities, such as my own. For the position in the Roman Catholic church, see Eoin de Bhaldraithe, 'Lay Abbots: Should We Return to the Earlier Church Practice?' *American Benedictine Review* 59 (2008) pp. 316–31.

The Abbot's Authority

Benedict takes over much of what is common tradition regarding the one who is 'first' in the community. Because he exercises a ministry of oversight, statements from scripture applied to the apostolic ministries are applied to the abbot.[11] Yet the abbot is answerable to God and has an immediate authority for his role and rule. He has on paper a high measure of freedom of action, but that freedom looks far less when placed in the context of the life of the community.

So, on the one hand, the abbot (*abbas*) enjoys in the Rule what seems to be an unchallengeable role. 'Insistence on the universal control exercised by the abbot ... is a characteristic' of the Rule.[12] Benedict 'puts enormous powers into the abbot's hands, powers practically untrammelled by any legal limitations'.[13] He is to be revered as one who is 'Christ's representative, since he is called by His name, the apostle saying: "You have received the spirit of adoption of sons, whereby we call Abba, Father"' (§2.2).[14] The disciple/monk is to obey his commands as if they were Christ's. There can be little doubt that this Christic foundation of the role of the abbot dissuaded early Anglican communities from placing themselves under the rule of Benedict; to the superficial observer, it can look like a pretension, at best self-reflectively innocent and neglectful of the malign tendencies of spiritual power. It can seem a licence for authoritarianism.

---

11 George Holzherr, *The Rule of Benedict: A Guide to Christian Living*, Dublin: Four Courts Press, 1994, p. 53.

12 Adalbert de Vogüé, *Community and Abbot in the Rule of Saint Benedict*, vol. 1, 1985, p. 411.

13 Christopher Butler OSB, *Benedictine Monachism: Studies In Benedictine Life And Rule*, London: Longmans, Green and Co., 1924, p. 186.

14 Addressing Christ as Father was once not as unusual as it has later become. In the Rule of the Master the 'Our Father' is addressed to Christ. See Basil Steidle, 'Heilige Vaterschaft', *Benedictinische Monatsschrift* 14 (1932), pp. 215–26 and 'Abba, Vater', *Benedictinische Monatsschrift* 16 (1934), pp. 89–101; Adalbert de Vogüé OSB, 'The Fatherhood of Christ', *Monastic Studies 5* (1968), pp. 45–58 and 'Experience of God and Spiritual Fatherhood', *Monastic Studies 9* (1972), pp. 83–97.

The role of the abbot is, however, one constructed on the base of the monastic tradition, itself based on figures and precepts drawn from the scriptures. Of particular importance is the image of Christ the shepherd and the moral advice found in the teachings of Christ and the pastoral epistles. This foundation has consequences for the understanding of obedience and of authority in the Community, and ensures that the office of the abbot is decentred in relation to the office of Christ the shepherd.

'The obedience shown to superiors is given to God' (§5.15). At first sight this seems authoritarian. That is a misleading impression, however, and an authoritarian approach does not correspond to Benedict's vision. As Kardong notes, there is 'reluctance to attribute unlimited authority to the abbot' in the rule.[15] The basis for this view of the abbot in relation to those under him is that of the shepherd, the physician and the steward; it is a Christological view, for the abbot is determined not only formally but also materially by the form of Christ. The abbot's authority is indeed limited, because it is from and in the service of Christ.[16]

What is significant is that this limit is found not in legal checks and balances, but in the way Christ is perceived in the life of the community and finds expression in its life. Notwithstanding the high theology of the abbot, it might be ventured that the authority he has emerges *in inverse proportion* to the independence with which he directs or commands. The gospel and example of Christ is the point of reference, and this means that the authority that emerges is significantly and systematically qualified. The abbot does have an authoritative place, but the context in which his control is expressed is such that it is far from what is usually characterised by authoritarianism.

---

15 Terence Kardong OSB, 'The Abbot as Leader', *American Benedictine Review* 42 (1991), pp. 53–72: p. 66.

16 Aquinata Böckmann OSB, *Christus hören: Exegetischer Kommentar zur Regel Benedikts, Teil 1: Prolog bis Kapitel 7*, St. Ottilien: Eos, 2011, pp. 292–3, 300.

The authority of the abbot is to have nothing in it which is of itself; it is to be oriented to the realisation of the purpose of the rule, which is to lead a community in the school of discipleship to be conformed to the passion of Christ; its purpose is to foster and nurture the making holy of Christian sinners.[17] The abbot is not to give way to his own preferences nor do simply what he wants (§63.2),[18] and he is under the same commitment to renounce his own will as his fellow monks. The object of his authority is the good and flourishing of the monks, whether strong or weak. Indeed he is to give attention to the individual needs and peculiarities as much as to the general requirements of the community's life, adapting himself to the ways of the monks (§2.31).

It is moreover an authority which is diversified. The fatherly care of the community (he is never termed a father of the monks, but of the monastery) is diversified among other officers who have responsibility in their own spheres. Each has his own responsibility which is in one sense, however, an extension of the abbot's.

The abbot represents Christ, but does so in relation to the Father; it is to the God of Our Lord Jesus Christ to whom he will answer (§2.38; 3.11). The background for this is that the abbot is directly bound to teach and do nothing that is not to be found in the teaching of the Lord, i.e. grounded in the holy scriptures (§2.4). The task of teaching according to the scriptures is a serious one (§§2.4–13; 64.2,9).

The abbot is not a substitute for Christ by way of a replacement, but rather an instantiation of relationship to Christ, in order to enable the living of the community. It is in this respect perhaps that the office has attracted aspects that look like sacramental order. The abbot is who he is by not being the one whose representative he is, for it is Christ who is the householder, the abbot, the father. His

17 Xavier McMonagle, OSB, 'The Service of Authority: The Abbot in the Rule of Benedict', *Cistercian Studies* 17 (1982), pp. 316–37.

18 '[T]he abbot is not to disturb the flock entrusted to him, nor make any unjust arrangements, as though he had the power to do whatever he wished.'

position is one which involves a radical de-centring and it is this very de-centring which secures this position.

It is possible to see that underlying the role of the abbot in his relationship to God, his standing in the place of Christ, there is a reflex of a particular Christological focus, namely the relation of the Son to the Father in the gospel of John. As von Balthasar notes, as the Rule progresses, the influence of two guides to the cenobitic way, Basil and Augustine makes itself felt: 'a whole Johannine atmosphere penetrates the Rule, especially towards the end.'[19]

Aquinata Böckmann has argued that the Rule is to be read in the first place as leading the monks to become like Christ; their commitment not to do their own will but that of Christ serves that end. Furthermore, this has the movement of Christ to us in obedience to the Father as its presupposition. This movement of Christ becomes the way of the monk, which leads to life. The abbot is then presented as the guarantee that the community is the place where this can be lived.[20] A modern commentator has remarked that it is the aim of the abbot to 'create a climate of meaning'[21] – one shot through with Christ. Yet this is so only because the abbot in community is as such decentred into the movement of Christ.

Obedience

This understanding of the abbot's authority is reflected in the nature of the community's obedience. Obedience is, of course, having a plausibility crisis in the modern world, not least in the light of the murderous abuse of the virtue in the conflicts of the last century. Obedience is, however, fundamental to the life of a community faithful to the gospel and under a monastic rule; it is so because of

19 Hans Urs von Balthasar, 'Johannine Themes in the Rule of St. Benedict and Their Meaning Today', *Cistercian Studies* 11 (1976), pp. 11–23.

20 Böckmann, *Christus hören*, pp. 306–7.

21 Casey and Tomlins, *Introducing Benedict's Rule*, p. 47.

what is entailed by following Christ, and of not holding on to one's own will. Some of the anxiety obedience evokes in contemporary society doubtless has to do with the countervailing emphasis on individual rights and fulfilment, often seen as conflicting with obedience owed to another. At best, obedience is construed as a form of moral constraint, and as a function of law and order. For Benedict, however, and indeed I would suggest for the Christian tradition generally, obedience is something foundational about graced humanity.[22] It is part of our calling to participate in the freedom and humility that come through Christ.

Obedience is indeed due to the abbot as to Christ; it is also due as to one whose life is to be after the example of Christ. This obedience is essentially one, but only the first is what derives from the institution of the *abbas*. The other flows from his role as a disciple among a group of disciples on the way. He presents the cross of Christ to his brethren, who will be weak and varied, by his commands and example, but also by his own frailty and limitations of which the Rule is clearly aware.

There is no doubt that in the Rule of Benedict there is a contrast between chapter 68, on the assignment of impossible tasks, and obedience in chapter 5, on obedience.[23] In the Rule of the Master, as for most of the early monastic tradition, a prompt and immediate response to the abbot's command was *de rigueur.* Cassian praises the unconditioned obedience of novices, who follow without discussion 'every command of the superior' as if they were 'given by God'; even 'when ... impossibilities are asked of them, they obey with such trusting devotion that they try to carry them wholeheartedly and without the slightest hesitation.'[24] In Benedict there is no question of such an obligation to the prompt obedience

22 See Holzherr, *Rule of Benedict*, pp. 80–5.

23 See Aquinata Böckmann, *Mit Christus zum Ziel: Exegetischer Kommentar zur Regel Benedikts*, Teil 3: Kapitel 53 bis 73, St. Ottilien: EoS, 2015, pp. 295–310.

24 John Cassian, *The Monastic Institutes: On the Training of a Monk and the Eight Deadly Sins*, tr. Jerome Bertram, London: Saint Austin, 1999: 4.10, p. 45.

of impossible commands. Indeed, one of the most far-reaching implications of what Benedict does in chapter 68 is to park the cult of heroic obedience. And what Benedict means by 'impossible' is not something physically absurd or impossible, such as standing on a roof for 24 hours or planting beans upside down, but what is impossible from the standpoint of the brother, whether in mind or body.[25] It is significant that in this chapter Benedict addresses how this relates to obedience, but also to the monk's well-being in community and its well-being in relation to him. Christian obedience can never be confined to simple submission to a command, but it has a root in the gift of love, given to someone in a particular place, which enables the monk to trust in the assistance of God because it is action done out of love.[26] Sometimes the monk is going to be faced with responsibilities or indeed commands which seem mightily uncongenial; an abbot may behave unreasonably; however, if a brother/sister is open and responsive, after they have explained reasonably why it is not good to do something and yet it remains what it is expected of them, then the love which is borne for the one from whom the command derives can place the 'impossible' demand in a context which will change its character. Brother Amos Schmidt has put this well:

> For if I succeed in taking the impossible command not only as a demand and what is more as an excessive one, but as a concern, whether of God, the abbot or the brothers, which I allow to be a 'concern' for me then the appearance of impossibility will perhaps fade. Such love is a grace, which the brother is to ask from God.[27]

---

25 Aquinata Böckmann OSB, 'Wenn einem Bruder Unmögliches aufgetragen wird (*Regula Benedicti cap. 68)', Erbe und Auftrag 68* (1992), pp. 5–21: p. 12.

26 Teresa Karin Fischediek, *Das Gehorsamsverständnis der 'Regula Benedicti': Der Gehorsam als Grundlage für ein exemplarisch christliches Gemeinschaftsleben,* St. Ottilien: Eos, 1993.

27 Amos Schmidt OSB, *Reflections on the Rule of Benedict*, Norwich: Canterbury Press, forthcoming. See also Böckmann, *Christus hören*, p. 290.

The issues in contemporary practice that this raises (abuse of power, self-delusion and bullying to name but three) are complex, but though it is possible to imagine cases when something is commanded which is contrary to divine faith or morals (and where no true obedience can be given), it remains true that a bare refusal, a refusal and nothing more, can never be a solution to a conflict.

The abbot is also under the same call and his authority is no less shaped by the obedience of Christ than that of the other brethren. He is a servant (*servus*) or rather *conservus* (§64.13) with the brethren who are also *servi*, all under the same Lord and all directed to the same end. He is bound to consult and moreover to consult the youngest, the most recently admitted of the monks (§3). All members of the community are called to participate in weighty decisions affecting the community because God often reveals what is better to the younger members. After listening to all the members, Benedict gives the final decision to the abbot but it is unusual for an abbot to decide against the community's choice.

The virtue that is sought and essential to the exercise of this authority, being such a focus of obedience, is *discretio* (§§2; 64.7–20), the 'mother of virtues' (§64.15). The abbot is to strive to be more loved than to be feared (§64.8),[28] to encourage the weak and to give the strong something to strive for. He drops the idea of competing in the path of holiness found in the Rule of the Master. In a famous phrase the abbot is advised to avoid being too severe, for if he is, by rubbing too hard to remove the rust, he may break the vessel (§64.13).

The clear relation of the abbot to Christ notwithstanding, there is no claim for an automatic justification for anything the abbot may fancy to do. In contrast to the earlier Rule of the Master, obedience without question is not part of the agenda.[29]

---

28 Echoing Augustine, *Rule*, 7.46; see midwestaugustinians.org/roots-of-augustinian-spirituality#ch7

29 This is a weakness in the presentation given by von Balthasar, 'Johannine Themes'.

> Obedient monks use their initiative and ideas to carry out tasks the abbot assigns, and the abbot assigns tasks that utilise the monks' abilities. This ideal, if practiced, results in the good of both the monk and the community.[30]

Thought there is no internal appeal, the abbot is accountable to the church outside; unusually among early rules, the Rule of Benedict makes explicit provision for the removal of a bad abbot (§64.4–5).

The place of obedience in cenobitism presupposes that it is a reality to be sought and desired elsewhere in the church and for reasons directly analogous to those which make it a good in the monastery: it is a gift which comes from the evangelical following of Christ. All the elect are called and enabled to the freedom and humility that come through Christ. What one has in obedience in the Rule of Benedict is a contextualised form of a virtue proper to the common life of the church of all the baptised, which applies to bishops as much as to anyone else.

Obedience is to Christ, but it is mediated by the abbot who stands in his stead, *vices Christi*, through whom the monk hears the word of God, but also by the scriptures, the silences and also the officers and the other monks. 'The main thrust is certain: obey the Christ who speaks through intermediaries.'[31] To follow Christ is to obey, but it is to obey in a context and a context in which the call is mediated through persons and situations. To obey is to hear the voice of God in one another and the community. It follows that obedience entails values such as reverence, handling with care and respect. It extends to material objects and to the work given; properly it is free of manipulation and exploitation.

Obedience is not therefore a matter of a compliance that is just external or subservient; to the latter Benedict attaches rather the

30 Jason King, 'The Exercise of Obedience and Authority in the Rule of Saint Benedict', *American Benedictine Review* 65 (2014), pp. 257–70: p. 264.

31 Böckmann, *Christus hören*, p. 387 (my translation).

vice of murmuring, the grip of self-will. Obedience is a gift that frees us from our own dependence on our own agendas, teachings and concerns and enables the will of God to be discerned in the persons and situations of the community and so enables us to listen to God rather than to the self; it is properly twinned with love, just as is the relation of the Son's obedience to the Father in John. Attention to external or even uncongenial directions may attend the practice of obedience, but that prepares for that time when it has become second nature, something internal and freely given and accepted, a virtue oriented towards the service of God and His love, the virtue of humility.

Obedience is mutual; it is not democratic (§71). There is a reciprocity without which the community can neither flourish nor function, nor can it hope for its end with God. Such reciprocal obedience is to obtain between the monks, but also between them and the abbot. The relation to the abbot is *sui generis*, because of his relation to Christ and of his responsibility, but the difference is not one of kind. The conduct of his office, to which the Rule gives so much attention, is based on the same scriptural foundation as that of the common obedience, for all are under the same rule and the same Christ.

Obedience is therefore a response that involves the rational intelligence of the monk and a consideration of his needs and gifts, as much as his frailties and sins. The attention of the abbot to individual needs and sins (§§2.24; 64.14) extends also to those aspects of a person where they have the capacity for initiative or freedom. In a modern context, that is likely to place an abbot in the position of one who holds back and channels energies rather than initiates.[32] Indeed, holding back and even questioning a monk's understanding of his vocations can be means of helping a community to grow and deepen its mission. Michael Casey uses the language of generativity to denote the fruit of such reciprocal listening and

---

32 Rembert Weakland OSB, 'The Abbot in a Democratic Society', *Cistercian Studies* 4 (1969), pp. 95–100.

obedience.[33] Just as the abbot may not direct any monk to do something that is contrary to the divine law (§2.4), so the monk is under no obligation to obey such a direction. Explicitly, the monk, when faced with an impossible command, is obliged to be open to the abbot about his difficulties (§68) trusting in the abbot to listen. 'His obedience is no mere compliance with orders but an obedience out of love, and he can trust in the assistance of God because it is action done out of love.'[34] One may say that all monks have a responsibility for the common obedience to the rule and to each other, such that one may speak of a 'co-responsibility', although different according to role in the community.[35]

Obedience is paradoxically neither intelligible nor fruitful when it is construed as a relationship between two individuals, of one to a superior. The abbot needs others to discern the will for a brother,[36] but also the brother needs others to discern God's will in the call to obedience and the grace of God to obey freely with a good will. An active community matrix is indispensable.

Can One Speak of Leadership in the Rule of Benedict?

Hitherto I have treated of the abbot in the context of a community marked by mutual obedience with a common end. Remarkably, no reference to the concept of leadership is present in this tradition. Appeal is frequently made to the Rule and to the wider monastic tradition for instruction about leadership; prioresses, abbots and abbots talk of leadership in their communities according to the Rule.

---

33 Michael Casey OCSO, *Strangers to the City: Reflections On The Beliefs And Values Of The Rule Of Saint Benedict*, Brewster, MA: Paraclete Press, 2005, p. 124.

34 Amos Schmidt OSB, *Reflections.*

35 Adelbert van der Wielen OSB, 'Coresponsibility According to the Rule of St Benedict', *Cistercian Studies* 9 (1974), pp. 348–353.

36 King, 'Exercise of Obedience', p. 269.

That is clear, but nowhere does the Rule itself use a term which calls to be translated by 'leader'.[37] The use of terms such as *abbas*, shepherd and steward indicate something rooted by the context of life in community under rule: that the role of leader is displaced, and constitutionally so: 'the flock is only committed to him, it is not his flock.'[38] The abbot and community do not relate either to one another or to Christ after the pattern of leader and led, commander and commanded. One might use such images to elucidate certain points, but they will not render the reality of the life of the community.

It might be asked why, questions of terminology apart, the concept of leadership is not one that arises in this context. The abbot does things that others called leaders do: he decides and directs, he executes decisions, admonishes, authorises and corrects, but the language of leadership is not current in the Rule.[39] It may be that the environs in which Benedictinism has lived and which always influence the way it finds expression have not needed such a concept, but perhaps it does now given the greater diversity of perspectives and cultures within the church and the pressing challenges that the church is facing. Possibly, but however much leadership may be a gift called for, however much it may be something to be sought and exercised with proper skill, its absence as a first-order concept may be instructive.

If we are to apply such a caution to the bishop, a different animal but with a similar office of oversight among the baptised, a shepherd and a steward, then one might pause before embracing a leadership model without systematic self-criticism, indeed a self-criticism which would have to be so self-critical as to raise a question as to the

---

37 E.g. Martin J. Burne OSB, 'Leadership in a Benedictine Community', in Philip Timko OSB (ed.), *Extending Our Benedictine Tradition*, Lisle, IL: Sacred Heart Convent and Saint Procopius Abbey, 1981, pp. 21–32; Kardong, 'Abbot as Leader'. Kardong is noticeably cool about the equation of abbot=leader.

38 Kardong, 'Abbot as Leader', p. 66.

39 I have found *regere* (to rule, govern) and cognates rendered by 'lead' in some recent translations of RB; e.g. by Placid Murray OSB, in Holzherr, *Rule of Benedict*, 2.37, p. 52.

rightness of the model employed. I would suggest that, whereas the language of leadership may serve the articulation of the church in various ways, confusing one who stands in some sort of vicarious relation to the source of life and guidance with a leader does not serve well the community of the baptised.

What we have in the Rule of Benedict and in the tradition of which it is the crux, is an ordering of the church of Christ for a particular kind of Christian, in and part of the greater church. In it the abbot has a role that is both institutional and spiritual, a position which the web of relations and counsels serves both to de-centre and to secure. This de-centring is however what locates and secures that authority. Moreover it is not a matter of a de-centring that is simply spiritual in the sense of moral behaviour, but of a de-centring that is institutionally embodied. It is not left to the private gifts or aptitudes to the occupier of the office.

The Christian church is a society in which the living reality of Christ takes social form. As such it is inevitably influenced by the ideas, patterns and practices of the environs in which it lives. However it has a life and an authority which is not one owed to such ideas, patterns and practices, but which derives from Christ and the Spirit, pre-eminently from Pentecost: 'It is ruled and authorised by the ascended Christ alone and supremely; it therefore has its own authority; and it is not answerable to any other authority that may attempt to subsume it'.[40] It is a distinct society. There is a paradox basic to it as a distinct society, that it has an authority of its own, but that it is derived from a reality which is not its own, namely the God of Jesus Christ. When it finds itself mirroring social realities not from that source, then it risks imperilling its capacity to live the reality of that social form. As a consequence – and this finds application in a variety of ecclesial forms of ministry and order – such a society expresses that paradox when that paradox is expressed

40 Oliver O'Donovan, *The Desire of the Nations: Rediscovering the Roots of Political Theology*, Cambridge: CUP, 1996, p. 159.

in accounts of its order and life, its ministry in and for community for example. In Benedictinism as I have expounded it, that is found in the relation of abbot and obedience in community. If, as I have suggested, it finds its basis in the community that is engendered in the obedience of Christ to the Father, that ministry can only find its basis here. One of the risks attending the use of leadership is that a concept arising from ideas, patterns and practices of a different kind of society can acquire a kind of first-order status and so displace that paradox which is vital to the society of the church.

It is a paradox which does not break down when structures or relations come under threat, but arguably comes into its own

> when one's hands are tied, when the mind can see no further, when everything seems dark, one can surrender into the hands of God and follow Christ who was obedient to death. He was obedient to Pontius Pilate, although Pilate was certainly not bothered about the will of God. It was just through this obedience, suffering obedience, that salvation came into the whole world. God's plan of salvation was, humanly speaking, not at all clear through Pontius Pilate. Did Christ recognise it? He trusted his Father, that he is so immense and yet carries through his will to save through very fragile intermediaries. That is what brings us to freedom and peace.[41]

41 Böckmann, *Christus hören*, p. 387 (my translation).

2.3 Senior Church Leadership and the Reformation

Charlotte Methuen

There is a sense in which the Reformation could be interpreted as the ultimate crisis in church leadership. Many of the questions that drove the Reformation centred around issues which, in the twenty-first century, we would categorise as having to do with leadership. Who had responsibility for the pastoral care and the teaching of the people in any given place? Who determined appointments in a parish or to a diocese? Who was responsible for providing structures and instruction that would support the spiritual health of the people of God? In different places, or in the same place at different times, answers to these questions might include, variously, the bishop of the diocese, the city council, a local prince or ruler, the pope, the king or the emperor.

The sixteenth century witnessed a radical reassessment of the vocation and task of the clergy; it saw the introduction of new methods and priorities for the education of clergy; it raised serious questions about the relationship between ecclesiastical and civic authority; and it experienced the rise of new models of ministry and new ways of thinking about authority, and thus about church leadership. All this added up to a new understanding of what the church was, but also to new ideas about who exercised authority in the church and how they did it. Many of the changes that came about during the sixteenth century still underlie our understandings of authority and proper leadership in the church today. The questions that led to those changes still resonate with some of the challenges that face leaders in today's church.

Calls for Change

Modern scholarship has revealed that many aspects of the life of the late medieval church were thriving. Popular piety was widespread, deeply rooted, and growing: many lay people were prepared to invest time, money and energy in supporting the church in order to try to ensure their salvation. As education became more accessible standards of education improved, and the printing trade made prayer books and Bibles more widely available. Lay people became more aware of their needs for support through the church and for teaching in questions of salvation. In some towns, citizens began to demand clergy who were able and willing to preach on the biblical texts; if the local bishop was unable or unwilling to appoint such preachers, the town council might take matters into its own hands. The establishment of posts for 'people's priests' in many late-medieval towns and cities in the German and Swiss lands witnesses to the considerable dissatisfaction felt by members of city and town councils with the way in which the church was being organised and led. Of course, not all lay people were in a position to call for change in the church. Moreover, many clergy were as exercised by the lack of biblical knowledge and the superstitious practices of the laity as they were by the ignorance and immorality of their fellow clergy. Increasingly, there were calls for a church in which both clergy and people were devout in practice and well educated in scripture and the fundamental tenets of the faith. There were calls too for a church which spoke to people – literally – in a language that they could understand, and not in the Latin of the university class; which taught them a theology that was rooted in the scriptures – that is, which preached a gospel, or evangelical (from *evangelium*, which means gospel) truth. In many ways, the medieval church, as Owen Chadwick long ago observed, was 'crying out for reformation',[1] but no-one quite seemed to know who should bring it about, or how.

---

1 Owen Chadwick, *The Reformation*, Penguin: Harmondsworth, 1964, p. 11.

One of the fundamental questions was that of who was responsible for – and indeed had the authority to – reform the church. In the late fourteenth century, the papacy had found itself in crisis after two contending popes emerged, one based in Avignon and the other in Rome. Efforts to resolve the Great Schism, as it came to be known, had for a short time led to a third claimant to papal authority. The existence of two, or even three, counter-claimants to papal authority had called into question the authority of the seat of Peter, and led to discussions about who (other than God) had the authority to rule over the pope, and thus to decide which of these competing candidates was in fact the vicar of Christ. One answer to this question was to locate ultimate authority over the church, not in the figure of the Pope, but in a council of all the bishops of the church. It was observed that the doctrinal statements of the early church had emerged from such councils – such as those of Nicaea, Constantinople and Chalcedon – and eventually it was another Council, that of Constance, which achieved the resolution of the Great Schism by appointing Pope Martin V as the single claimant to the See of Rome. However, the Council instructed that he and his successors should call a general council of all bishops every ten years. Mostly his successors did not do so, preferring to exercise their rule of the church through the curia. Nonetheless, the Great Schism bequeathed the idea of conciliar authority to the Western church. It also left an enduring legacy of questions about the locus of authority in the church; these would have consequences in the Reformation and afterwards.

Questions about the credibility of ecclesiastical leadership did not emerge only in relation to the papacy. Examples of the appointment of untrained and inappropriate clergy to ecclesiastical posts abounded. These were generally associated with a multiplication of offices which increased the personal wealth and power of the holder, but which led to absenteeism and often resulted in a disinvestment and lack of interest for ministry locally. From 1518 to 1522, Thomas Wolsey was concurrently Archbishop of York (1514–1530) and Bishop of Bath and Wells; subsequently he was also Prince-Bishop of Durham (1523–1529), and Bishop of Winchester (1529–1530). A Dutch cardinal collected over a hundred benefices of various kinds, stretching across two dioceses, was bishop of two dioceses, and drew an annual income of at least 26,000 ducats. Such examples served to highlight the problem of leadership in the late-medieval church. These men were often significant players in another arena: at court, in the diplomatic or political world, in Rome. Cardinal Wolsey was Chancellor of all England: until he fell out of favour, he exercised an important leadership role in Henry VIII's England, but as Archbishop of York, his main energies were not directed at his diocese nor his province: indeed he first visited York in 1529, 15 years after his appointment. The late medieval church offers many examples of ecclesiastical leaders whose primary interests, efforts and attention were directed away from the daily running of their parishes, cathedrals and dioceses. Many of them amassed considerable political power and personal wealth. As laity became more educated and better able to articulate their needs and their demands, this situation became increasingly intolerable to them.

One of those who articulated – and by articulating also spread – such critical opinions was the humanist scholar Desiderius Erasmus. Erasmus was incensed by bishops and abbots who did not take their spiritual responsibilities seriously. In his satirical work *In Praise of Folly* (1509) he wrote of the bishops:

> If any of them would consider what their Alb should put them in mind of, to wit a blameless life; what is meant by their forked mitres, whose each point is held in by the same knot, we'll suppose it a perfect knowledge of the Old and New Testaments; what those gloves on their hands, but a sincere administration of the Sacraments, and free from all touch of worldly business; what their crosier, but a careful looking after the flock committed to their charge; what the cross borne before them, but victory over all earthly affections – these,

> I say, and many of the like kind should anyone truly consider, would he not live a sad and troublesome life?[2]

Bishops, in Erasmus's view, had lost sight of their true function, the preaching and teaching of Scripture, and the administration of the sacraments; they had forgotten their responsibility to pursue a holy life, and had instead become caught up in the intricacies of worldly politics and concerns. They were not, in any proper sense, spiritual leaders. Erasmus's critique would be echoed by Martin Luther. The two men were part of a mood of anti-clericalism which was united (if not always entirely fair) in its denouncement of the immorality and spiritual incompetence of the church's leaders. But the reform of the episcopate was felt by many to be an urgent need, and across the Western Church some bishops set themselves to respond to this need. With the support of Ferdinand and Isabella, king and queen of Spain, the Franciscan Francisco Ximénez de Cisneros, appointed Archbishop of Toledo in 1495, introduced a humanist reform of clerical education and church practices, including the forbidding of the sale of indulgences. Guillaume Briçonnet, appointed Bishop of Meaux in 1516 under the influence of the French king's sister, Marguerite de Navarre, was active in reforming his diocese, appointing the Humanist Jacques Lefèvre d'Etaples to assist in Bible translation and Lutheran clergy to preach the gospel; he was denounced by French Franciscans and condemned by the Sorbonne theologians. Christoph von Utenheim, bishop of Basel from 1502, implemented reforms in his diocese and appointed reforming, evangelical clergy to preach in his diocese. These clergy then gained the support of the city council, which formally introduced the Reformation in 1529; the bishop was ousted from his see. Reform-minded episcopal leadership could (and indeed still can) have unexpected results.

---

2 Desiderius Erasmus, *In Praise of Folly*, tr. John Wilson, Mineola, NY: Dover, 2003, p. 55.

Martin Luther

In the late-medieval church, canonical law and the practices of the sacramental system had generated the sense that clergy and religious, however, worldly and unspiritual their lifestyles, were spiritually superior to the most devout lay person. This division between the spiritual and the temporal infuriated Martin Luther. In reality, he wrote in a treatise addressed 'to the Christian Nobility of the German Nation' (1520),

> those who are now called 'spiritual', that is, priests, bishops, or popes, are neither different from other Christians nor superior to them, except that they are charged with the administration of the word of God and the sacraments.[3]

Luther was convinced that spiritual authority lay not only with clergy, but with the whole people of God, and he argued that a lay person guided by the Holy Spirit was as capable of interpreting Scripture and understanding God's word as the Pope. Therefore, he concluded, 'it is the duty of every Christian to espouse the cause of the faith, to understand and defend it, and to denounce every error.'[4] However, although Luther was convinced that every Christian had a role to play in the propagation of gospel truth, he was nonetheless adamant that a specific (and normally male) person must be appointed to preach the gospel and celebrate the sacraments in the context of parish worship. As he explained in his lectures on Titus, 'Christians all have a priesthood, but they do not all have the priestly function. Although all can teach and exhort, nevertheless one ought to do so, and the other ought to listen.'[5] The common priesthood shared by all believers did not, in Luther's view, mandate all Christians to a public ministry.

---

3 Martin Luther, *To the Christian Nobility of the German Nation*, Luther's Works, vol. 44, Philadelphia, PA: Fortress, 1966, pp. 123–217: p. 130.

4 Luther, *To the Christian Nobility*, p. 136.

5 Luther, *Lectures on Titus*, Luther's Works, vol. 29, St. Louis, MO: Concordia, 1968, pp. 4–90: p. 16.

Luther's conviction that every believer stood equal before God, and that all believers were called to propagate gospel truth, has come to be known as the doctrine of the priesthood of all believers. His emphasis on the equal spiritual authority of all Christians raised important questions about the legitimacy of papal authority and of the ecclesiastical hierarchy, and it also had implications for the leadership and organisation of parish churches. Luther argued, for instance, that local clergy should be appointed with some attention to the local community:

> when a bishop consecrates [someone as a parish priest] it is nothing else than that in the place and stead of the whole community, all of whom have like power, he takes a person and charges him to exercise this power on behalf of the others.[6]

Indeed, in some circumstances, Luther suggested, a community might appoint their priest themselves:

> Suppose a group of earnest Christian laymen were taken prisoner and set down in a desert without an episcopally ordained priest among them. And suppose they were to come to a common mind there and then in the desert and elect one of their number, whether he were married or not, and charge him to baptise, say mass, pronounce absolution, and preach the gospel. Such a man would be as truly a priest as though he had been ordained by all the bishops and popes in the world.[7]

It was important, in Luther's view, that those charged with preaching the word of God were able to fulfil this office. For, he believed, 'the entire spiritual estate—all the apostles, bishops, and priests—has been called and instituted only for the ministry of the Word.'[8] For Luther, therefore, the proper task of a priest or bishop must be centred on the Word of God.

---

6 Luther, *To the Christian Nobility*, p. 128.

7 Luther, *To the Christian Nobility*, p. 128.

8 Luther, *The Freedom of a Christian*, Luther's Works vol. 31, Philadelphia, PA: Fortress, 1957, pp. 333–77: p. 346.

Other tasks could offer a distraction to that focus. 'How,' Luther asked 'can a man rule and at the same time preach, pray, study, and care for the poor?'[9] The political expectations placed on many bishops were, in his view, unreasonable, and these, together with other organisational tasks, should if possible be delegated. The practices of medieval religion were also problematic in this respect, since Luther saw them as a distraction from a proper focus on the Word:

> The duty of a priest is to preach, and if he does not preach he is as much a priest as a picture of a man is a man. Does ordaining such babbling priests make one a bishop? Or blessing churches and bells? Or confirming children? Certainly not. Any deacon or layman could do as much. It is the ministry of the Word that makes the priest and the bishop.[10]

For Luther, the appropriate leadership of the church included the discernment of the proper tasks of bishops and priests, and the establishment of structures which would enable them to carry out those tasks without distraction. These tasks might include those which would later come to be classified under the term *episcopé*: which in the case of the Pope was the 'care of all Christendom',[11] and in the case of bishops the oversight of church life in a larger area.

Luther, however, although he found himself dealing with a territorial church, was not wedded to the idea of the territorial episcopate, which he did not believe to be biblical. Expounding Titus 1.5, he observed that

> it was Paul's ordinance that he should select 'elders' (in the plural) in each city, and they are called bishops and elders. Therefore at the time of the apostles every city had numerous bishops.[12]

---

9 Luther, *To the Christian Nobility,* p. 166.

10 Luther, *The Babylonian Captivity of the Church*, Luther's Works, vol. 36, Philadelphia, PA: Fortress, 1959, pp. 3–126: p. 115.

11 Luther, *To the Christian Nobility,* p. 159.

12 Luther, *Titus,* p. 16.

The ideal, Luther suggested, was that these bishops or elders – who in his view might better be termed 'inspectors' or 'visitors' – should know their people well enough to exhort them to a better life:

> Every city ought to have many bishops, that is, inspectors or visitors. Such an inspector should be the parish clergyman along with the chaplain, so that they may share the duties and see how people live and what is taught. He would see who is a usurer, and then he would speak the Word of healing and correction.[13]

Indeed, in Luther's view, the local pastor and the schoolteacher were the primary 'inspectors' of the congregation's behaviour: 'pastors and schoolteachers are the lowly, but daily, permanent, eternal judges who anathematise without interruption, that is, fend off the devil and his raging.'[14]

Nonetheless, a further level of oversight proved necessary. In the late 1520s, Luther, in conjunction with Philip Melanchthon, instigated a system of visitations or inspections of parishes across Saxony. The 'Electoral Instruction' for the 1527 visitation made clear that the authority behind the process was that of the Elector of Saxony, who, by virtue of his authority as the ruler of the state, had introduced and effected the visitation. The authority of the visitors, in both their spiritual and their secular capacity, therefore derived from that of the Elector:

> For although his Electoral Grace is not commanded to teach and rule spiritually, nevertheless he is responsible, as secular ruler, to maintain things so that dissension, bands, and disorder do not arise among the subjects.[15]

---

13 Luther, *Titus*, p. 17.

14 Luther, *On the Councils and the Church*, Luther's Works 41, Philadelphia, PA: Fortress, 1966, pp. 9–178: p. 134–5.

15 Luther, 'Preface to the Instructions for Visitors', quoted in Lewis W. Spitz, 'Luther's Ecclesiology and his Concept of the Prince as *Notbischof*', *Church History* 22 (1953), pp. 113–141: pp. 131–2.

For Luther, in the absence of suitable bishops, such 'things' included the organisation of the church and the appointment of pastors. Although Luther seems to have been quite happy to see the appointment of suitable candidates as evangelical bishops and continued to regard the prince in this role strictly as an 'emergency bishop',[16] the pattern by which the local territorial ruler, whether prince or city council, *de facto* held responsibility for the organisation of the church in that territory in fact became the norm in many, if not most, Lutheran contexts. If a final arbiter were needed, Luther suggested that a council – which he understood as a kind of appeal court – be appealed to:

> the council is the great servant or judge in this empire and law. Yet when the emergency has passed, it has done its duty—just as, in temporal government, the supreme, great judges have to help when the lower, secondary courts prove too weak to cope with an evil, until the case is at last brought before the highest, greatest court, the diet, which cannot meet forever either, but must adjourn after the emergency is over and again leave matters to the lower courts.[17]

Leadership in the church was for Luther a matter of ensuring that the pastors of the church were equipped to preach gospel truth effectively, and that their message was being received by their people. Luther did not specify a particular polity or ministerial and ecclesiastical structure of ministry through which this should take place, although he did suggest guidelines for visitations, and both he and, in particular, Philip Melanchthon, were involved in the introduction of the Reformation and the concomitant reforms of schools and universities in a number of German territories. In the German lands, the decision to introduce the Reformation – to ensure vernacular preaching and worship together with the availability of the scriptures in the vernacular, to give communion in both kinds,

16 See Spitz, 'Luther's Ecclesiology'.

17 Luther, *On the Councils and the Church*, p. 134.

to dissolve monasteries and convents, and reform the school system, to determine theology rooted in the gospel, and to allow married clergy – was generally taken by the civic authority of the territory, be that a prince or a city council. By introducing the Reformation, leadership of the church in these areas generally passed to the civic authority, delegated to senior pastors, who in many cases were also the professors or teachers of theology at the local university or high school. Bishops largely disappeared, only to reappear in the twentieth century. In Scandinavia, in contrast, in the context of a Reformation introduced by the crown, Lutheran churches continued to be led by a reformed episcopate, understood as senior pastors exercising a territorial ministry of oversight, although in Norway and Denmark these bishops were renamed superintendents, seen as a more accurate translation of the Latin meaning of the Greek term *episcopos.* The continuation of this ministry of oversight in part recognised that the leadership of a national church required a national structure.

John Calvin

In Geneva, the city council was instrumental in introducing the Reformation in 1536. However, although the city council continued to maintain that responsibility for church leadership ultimately lay in its hands, Geneva's reformers – and in particular John Calvin – disagreed. The models that Luther was prepared to accept seemed to Calvin to cede too much authority over the church to the temporal and civic powers. The conflict over the level of power that should be held by the city council would run on for the next 20 years; against Calvin's wishes, the town council retained the right of excommunication until 1555. Under Calvin's guidance, Geneva's pastorate was entirely reorganised on what Calvin believed to be biblical grounds. He offered a radical revision of the three-fold ministry of bishops, priests and deacons, substituting instead a four-fold ministry of doctors or theological teachers, pastors, elders and deacons. As he commented in the *Institutes*, 'this human ministry which God uses to govern the church is the chief sinew by which believers are held together in one body.'[18]

For Calvin, the ministry of the Word was restricted to the first two of these categories, doctors or teachers and pastors. The teachers were in charge of scriptural interpretation, 'to keep doctrine whole and pure among believers',[19] whilst the responsibilities of pastors included a whole range of functions: 'discipline, or administering the sacraments, or warnings and exhortations'[20] as well as the proclamation of the gospel through preaching and scriptural interpretation. Pastors should, except in cases of emergency, restrict their ministry to their own parish, and 'content with his own limits, should not break over into another man's province.'[21] Calvin saw here a parallel between the New Testament ministries of prophet, which he thought similar to that of teacher, and apostle, which he compared to that of the pastor, but he noted too that New Testament terminology had been less specific in designating office than later use might suggest:

> in indiscriminately calling those who rule the church 'bishops', 'presbyters', 'pastors', and 'ministers', I did so according to Scriptural usage, which interchanges these terms. For to all who carry out the ministry of the Word it accords the title of 'bishops'.[22]

In particular, when related to the preaching office, the terms presbyter and bishop were for Calvin equivalent. However, Calvin did recognise also the ministry of elders, who, he believed, were those who exercised the Pauline ministry of governance: 'Each church, therefore, had from its beginning a senate, chosen from godly, grave, and holy men, which had jurisdiction over the

18 John Calvin, *Institutes of the Christian Religion*, tr. Ford Lewis Battles, Louisville, KY: Westminster John Knox, 1960, IV.3.2.

19 Calvin, *Institutes*, IV.3.4.

20 Calvin, *Institutes*, IV.3.4.

21 Calvin, *Institutes*, IV.3.7.

22 Calvin, *Institutes*, IV.3.8.

correcting of faults.'[23] Similarly, each church had a responsibility for care for the poor, and this was entrusted to deacons, of whom there were two sorts: 'one to serve the church in administering the affairs of the poor; the other, in caring for the poor themselves.'[24] Women, thought Calvin, 'could fill no other public office than to devote themselves to the care of the poor.'[25]

Those responsible for running the Genevan church worked together in two main groupings: the 'Venerable Company' or college of pastors and theologians, which exercised authority in questions of theology and the practical running of the church such as the selection of pastors (Calvin was its moderator until shortly before his death); and the consistory, made up of pastors and elders, which was responsible for church discipline, including the regulation of the conduct of members of the church – i.e. Geneva's population. The college of pastors was modelled on the pattern of ministry in the early church, as Calvin understood it, in which each city 'had a college of presbyters, who were pastors and teachers,' and 'each college was under one bishop for the preservation of its organisation and peace.' However, this 'bishop' was not higher in rank: 'While he surpassed the others in dignity, he was subject to the assembly of his brethren,' and he could delegate his responsibilities to other presbyters.[26] The bishop, thought Calvin, had also supervised the apportioning of the resources of the church to pay the clergy, to ensure that church buildings were kept in good repair and to distribute alms to the poor. This, Calvin believed, was part of the responsibility of the college of pastors, with alms being distributed through the deacons. New pastors were (at least in theory) to be elected by the people under the supervision of the pastors:

> this call of a minister is lawful according to the Word of God, when those who seemed fit are created by the consent and

23 Calvin, *Institutes*, IV.3.9.

24 Calvin, *Institutes*, IV.3.9.

25 Calvin, *Institutes*, IV.3.9.

26 Calvin, *Institutes*, IV.4.2.

> approval of the people; moreover, that other pastors ought to preside over the election in order that the multitude may not go wrong either through fickleness, through evil intentions, or through disorder.[27]

In this way, 'neither were the clergy allowed to appoint whom they wished, nor was it necessary for them to follow the foolish desires of the people.'[28] In practice, Geneva's pastors were appointed by the college of pastors and the appointment confirmed by the city council. After examination of the candidate's doctrine and morals, ordination was by the pastors through laying on of hands.

Calvin did not think that any particular form of church leadership was necessary for salvation. However, he emphasised that just as 'some form of organisation is necessary in all human society to foster the common peace and maintain concord,' some form of organisation and procedure must also be necessary in the church. It was necessary that 'those in charge know the rule and law of good governing,' but also that 'the people who are governed become accustomed to obedience to God and to right discipline.'[29] Unlike Luther, Calvin was adamant that structures of church leadership should be independent of the civic authority. In particular, he deplored the 'disorderly practice' which 'gave the princes occasion to appropriate to themselves the presentation of bishops' instead of seeking the approval of the people.[30] This, for Calvin, had been the root of many of the abuses of the church. Nonetheless, he recognised that there might be overlaps between church and civic governance: in Geneva many of the elders were city councillors, and in many ways the governance of the church was integrated with – and pursued the same aims as – civic government in its attempts to achieve an orderly and moral society. The structures of church

27 Calvin, *Institutes*, IV.3.15.

28 Calvin, *Institutes*, IV.4.12.

29 Calvin, *Institutes*, IV.10.28.

30 Calvin, *Institutes*, IV.5.3.

leadership were separate from those of temporal leadership, but they were to be seen as complementary. Calvin's vision for the leadership of the church was much more consciously synodical than Luther's; he attempted to ensure that authority was shared between pastors and at least some of the people. In theory, at least, this was a system which intended that power could not become concentrated in the hands of one person or even one exclusive group of people. A particular interest in the reform of church leadership structures in order to separate them from the influence of the civic authorities would become a feature of much Calvinist reform of the Church.

The English Reformation

In England, as in Scandinavia, the Reformation was introduced under the auspices of the crown. Unlike the situation in the German or Swiss lands, in which bishops were often seen as a challenge to the temporal authority and as opponents to the introduction of the Reformation, the appointment of Thomas Cranmer as Archbishop of Canterbury meant than in England, bishops were closely involved both in introducing and in resisting the Reformation. In the view of the leaders of the church in England, what was needed to improve church leadership was not a revised structure for the ministry, as Calvin had introduced into Geneva, but a reformed episcopate.

Reforms to the episcopate were already being suggested in the draft canons put forward by the Canterbury convocation which met in conjunction with the Reform Parliament in 1529. Canon 1 instructed that the bishops should 'diligently carry out the things which are written below as well as other things which pertain to their office.'[31] These included their presence in their cathedral churches to celebrate mass at Christmas, Easter and Pentecost and in Holy Week, their consecration of oil on Maundy Thursday, their presence in their

31 Gerald Bray (ed.), *The Anglican Canons, 1529–1947*, Church of England Record Society 6, Woodbridge: Boydell, 1998, p. 2/3 (the Latin text is given on the even-numbered pages, the English translation on the odd).

dioceses 'reforming monasteries and residences, disciplining the clergy and people, eradicating heresies, and sowing the Word of Life in the Lord's field.'[32] Bishops should 'take much greater care than hitherto' in the appointment of clergy, remove incompetent clergy promptly, enforce residence, encourage the education of the clergy and require preaching.[33] Although the 1529 Canons were never officially enacted, their description of the proper ministry of a bishop remained influential.

In 1534, ultimate authority in the English church passed to King Henry VIII and his successors, subject only to God, who through the Act of Supremacy was given comprehensive powers to rule the church by means of parliament. However, the place of bishops in the leadership of the English church was to be maintained. Also in 1534, a procedure for the selection and election of bishops was drawn up, and the Suffragan Bishops Act allowed for the nomination by the diocesan bishop of up to two suffragan bishops in each diocese, to share in the episcopal duties of the diocesan. It also specified that such a bishop 'for the better maintenance of his dignity, might have two benefices with cure.'[34] Multiplicity of offices was decreased, but not yet suppressed; in fact little use was made of the Act, with only twelve suffragans being established under Henry VIII. With the dissolution of the monasteries, the 17 late-medieval dioceses in England became 22, and all were given a secular constitution, with a chapter headed up by a Dean. Bishops retained their seats in the House of Lords and were thus integrated into the government of England. It was clear that despite the rejection of Papal authority, bishops and dioceses would continue as the primary instrument of the organisation and governance of the English church.

Henry VIII's bishops seem to have taken their spiritual responsibilities seriously. In 1537, the 'prelates' of the English church, including

---

32 Ibid., pp. 2/3–6/7

33 Ibid., p. 4/5

34 Gerald Bray (edn), *Documents of the English Reformation*, Cambridge: James Clarke; corrected reprint 2004, p. 117.

bishops and archdeacons, published *The institution of a Christen man conteynynge the exposytion or interpretation of the commune Crede, of the seuen Sacramentes, of the .x. commandementes, and of the Pater noster, and the Aue Maria, iustyfication [and] purgatory,* the so-called Bishops' Book, a catechetical work. However, they shared with (indeed were sometimes subject to) official government-appointed visitors in the task of ensuring that decisions made by the king and his advisers had been implemented. Thus the instructions contained in the Henrician Injunctions of 1536 and 1538, including the removal of lights, the suppression of images, the setting up of English Bibles, and the regular teaching of the Lord's prayer, the ten commandments and the creed in the vernacular were to be implemented by parish clergy, but both royal visitors and bishops were charged to see that this had been done. Moreover, despite the undoubted importance of the bishops, it was the influence of Thomas Cromwell – a layman, and certainly not a bishop, who was appointed vicegerent for spirituals (effectively vicar general) of the Church of England in 1535 – which was most significant in shaping the direction of the English church in the latter part of the 1530s, and the King himself played a central role in the conservative backlash of the early 1540s. His corrected version of the Bishops' Book, *A necessary doctrine and erudicion for any chrysten man set furth by the kynges maiestye of Englande,* the so-called King's Book, was published in 1543. The king and his ministers would continue to play a central role in determining the direction and doctrine of the English church.

This pattern continued under Edward VI. Bishops continued to be appointed, and there was no change to the three-fold ministry. Indeed the preface to the 1550 ordinal, affirmed that 'It is evident unto all men, diligently reading Holy Scripture, and ancient authors, that from the Apostles' time, there hath been these orders of Ministers in Christ's church – bishops, priests, and deacons.'[35] The ordinal also affirmed that these were not private, but public offices,

---

35 Ibid., p. 277.

so that 'no man by his own private authority, might presume to execute any of them, except that he were first called, tried, examined, and known, to have such equalities, as were requisite for the same.'[36] The ordinal required the bishop to teach and instruct his people according to scripture; to pray for understanding that he might 'teache and exhorte with wholesome doctrine' and 'banishe and drive away al erronious and straunge doctryne, contrary to god's worde'; to show a good example by living 'soberly, ryghteouslye, and godly in thys world'; and to 'maintain and set forward (as muche as shal lie in you) quietnesse, peace, and love, emonge al men.'[37] To this end, the bishop was also charged with the exercise of discipline, that 'suche as be unquiete, disobedyente, and criminous within your Diocesse, [you shall] correcte and punishe, accordyng to suche aucthoritie, as ye have by gods worde, and as to you shal be committed, by the ordinaunce of thys realme.'

Under Edward VI, bishops were appointed by the king. The 1547 Election of Bishops Act discontinued what had long been largely a charade of having bishops and archbishops elected by the dean and chapter of the diocese, instead giving the king the right 'when any archbishopric or bishopric be void, [to] confer the same to any person whom the King shall think meet.' Decisions about the church were made centrally, after consultation between Archbishop, bishops and theological advisors such as the reformers Martin Bucer and Peter Martyr Vermigli, and confirmed by parliament, who might also impose changes (such as the black rubric, which instructed communicants to kneel when receiving the eucharistic elements, 'for a sygnificacion of the humble and gratefull acknowledgyng of the benefites of Chryst, geven unto the woorthye receiver'[38]). The implementation of the sweeping changes to liturgical practice and

---

36 Ibid., pp. 277–278.

37 1550 Ordinal, online at: www.justus.anglican.org/resources/bcp/1549/Bishops_1549.htm (accessed 8/11/2015).

38 1552 Book of Common Prayer, online at www.justus.anglican.org/resources/bcp/1552/Communion_1552.htm (accessed 8/11/2015).

the ordering of church buildings were imposed by parliamentary act and through the use of injunctions, backed up, as under Henry VIII, by a nationally organised system of visitations. Bishops were certainly involved in carrying this out, but they were not always the prime movers. Indeed, diocesan structures suffered from neglect during this period of rapid change. This trend was reversed by Mary I with the help of her Archbishop of Canterbury, Reginald Pole. The reintroduction of Catholicism into England led to a reordering of diocesan structures, and several cathedrals received their first secular statutes during Mary's reign.

Under Elizabeth I, who would reign for 45 years, the English church entered into a period of relative stability, and found itself in a better position both to establish lasting changes, and to consider questions of structure and leadership. The Queen and her ministers – generally including the Archbishop of Canterbury, although Elizabeth got on better with some than with others – continued to exercise considerable authority in the church, and policy ultimately came from them. However, they were very aware of the need to ensure that the structures and ministries of the church were effective. In particular, the authority of Queen and parliament in the church was challenged by the growing influence of Calvinist theology and polity, and this would become a more urgent problem in the course of the 1570s, although Calvin's vision of an independent church would not become reality in England. The attention to questions of leadership can be seen in the 1571 canons, which specified the responsibilities of a range of different ministries in the church, both ordained and lay, including bishops; cathedral deans; archdeacons; chancellors, commissaries and other diocesan officials, who played an important role in supervising the parish clergy and ensuring their good behaviour; churchwardens and 'sidemen'; preachers; schoolmasters; and 'patrons and proprietors'.[39] The canons sought to clarify expectations relating to the education of clergy, to enforce

39 See Bray, *Anglican Canons*, pp. 172/173–2004/205

the residence of parish clergy, to abolish the holding of multiple offices, and to regulate excommunication. The 1571 canons were revised twice under Elizabeth and were strongly influential on the canons of 1603/4, which would remain the legal foundation of the Church of England until 1969.

The Reformation in Scotland

Although Calvinist theology was influential in the English church under Elizabeth, its proponents did not succeed in introducing a Genevan polity into England. That battle was fought in Scotland, where the Reformation was introduced into Scotland in 1559 with a much more explicitly Calvinist theology and a polity also influenced by the Reformed models that John Knox had encountered in Geneva and Frankfurt. The Book of Discipline of 1560, largely drafted by Knox, envisaged ministers who would be elected and appointed by their congregations after examination by 'men of soundest judgment', usually in a university town. It divided Scotland into dioceses, each under the care of a superintendent, who was to be diligent in visiting the parishes under his care, and who might also examine pastors. Knox's system ran into problems, mainly because of the lack of trained ministers, but also because some of the Scottish bishops proved themselves diligent in introducing the Reforms, and because many of the Scottish nobility were reluctant to cede their rights of patronage. In 1572, the episcopate was restored, with bishops appointed but not consecrated and subject to assembly. However, this development attracted considerable opposition and in 1578, under the influence of Andrew Melville, the Second Book of Discipline proposed a system of government by ministers and laity through an ascending series of Church Courts: local Kirk Sessions; regional Presbyteries and Synods; and a national General Assembly presided over by a Moderator elected annually. In 1592 this Presbyterian system was endorsed by the Scottish Parliament. However, bishops, later known as commissioners, nominated by James VI, continued not only to exist but to sit in Parliament. When, in 1603, James VI became also James I of England, many expected a return to episcopacy in Scotland, and when that expectation proved a reality, many opposed it. In the course of the seventeenth century, the resulting struggles over ecclesiastical polity would tear apart church and country in both England and Scotland. Attempts to hold together the different systems would give rise to suggestions for a synodical episcopacy, such as that put forward by James Ussher in the later seventeenth century. However, by the end of the seventeenth century, England's ecclesiastical polity was Episcopal, whilst Scotland's was Presbyterian. Calvin's question of where authority for leadership the church should rest had been answered in very different ways.

Conclusion

The sixteenth century raised massive questions about the locus and form of church leadership. The practical questions which are faced by senior church leaders today are not the same questions which faced their predecessors during the Reformation. However, many of the underlying – and conflicting – assumptions about the proper leadership of the church which shape contemporary answers to those questions were forged in the debates of the sixteenth century.

2.4 Changing Models of Episcopacy, 1800 to the Present

Jeremy Morris

Pervasive anxiety about the nature of leadership today – an anxiety which runs through political life and business administration as well as the Church of England – surely tells us as much about the pathology of our self-perceptions as it does about the actual context in which leadership has to be exercised. There is nothing intrinsically more complicated about our lives than there was about the lives of many of our forebears, at least as they were experienced and described. We might like to think it is otherwise, but a glance at the testimony of those who lived in earlier centuries gives us no liberty to think that they conceived of their lives as in some sense simple or predictable, or that the difficulties they faced were in any meaningful sense less intense than ours. Indeed, one of the paradoxes of modernisation theory – or rather, one of its internal contradictions – is that it perceives a simplicity and predictability in the past, in one breath, that it instantly imagines away in another when it supposes the advance of 'rational', or predictable, streamlined technologies of control. A discussion of episcopal leadership over the last 200 years should not, therefore, confine itself to the supposed phenomenon itself (that is, to what constitutes episcopal leadership properly conceived), but to the 'pathology' that gives rise to the concern in the first place. It says as much about our anxiety about leadership, in other words, as it does about the actual exercise of it.

Anyone looking for a theoretical discussion of the sources, nature and shape of episcopal leadership will find thin gruel in much

Anglican discourse of the last two centuries. It was not until the twentieth century that mechanisms existed (in church commissions and reports, for example) to identify problems and pursue related lines of enquiry. There was, of course, running controversy on the nature of the ordained ministry, which included significant discussion of episcopal authority, and the main points of this story have been noted by a variety of writers.[1] They note that the early-nineteenth-century understanding of the episcopate placed an emphasis as much on the legal authority of rightly-commissioned ministers, and especially bishops, as it did on the intrinsic spiritual authority derived from apostolic succession, and that it was a Tractarian innovation to emphasise the latter at the expense of the former.[2] They recognise that, under the influence of Tractarianism and then of Anglo-Catholicism more widely, the balance of Anglican views of ministry overall then shifted, so that even moderate proposals for church reunion – such as that which eventually became known as the Lambeth Quadrilateral – carried something of the imprint of the renewed emphasis on episcopacy and succession,[3] even though all this happened at a time when the historical claims on which the Tractarian view rested were becoming more contested.[4] And they describe how, later still, under the influence of ongoing patristic scholarship, elements of continental Catholicism, and ecumenical dialogue, a certain re-imagining of ministerial authority could take place, re-emphasising the apostolicity of the whole Church and the

---

1 See Paul Avis, *Anglicanism and the Christian Church: Theological Resources in Historical Perspective*, London: Continuum, new edn., 2002; Mark Chapman, *By What Authority? Authority, Ministry and the Catholic Church*, London: DLT, 1997.

2 P. B. Nockles, *The Oxford Movement in Context: Anglican High Churchmanship 1760–1857*, Cambridge: CUP, 1994, esp. pp. 146–183.

3 See the essays in J. Robert Wright (ed.), *Quadrilateral at One Hundred*, Oxford: Mowbray, 1988; on Evangelical opposition to Tractarianism, see P. Toon, *Evangelical Theology 1833–1856: A Response to Tractarianism*, London: Marshall, Morgan & Scott, 1979, and M. Wellings, *Evangelicals Embattled: Responses of Evangelicals in the Church of England to Ritualism, Darwinism and Theological Liberalism 1890–1930*, Milton Keynes: Paternoster Press, 2003.

4 F.D. Maurice's views on the threefold ministry, and particularly episcopacy, are to be found in *The Kingdom of Christ*, II, London: Macmillan, 4th edn., 1891, pp. 171–5; there is a summary in J.N. Morris, *F.D. Maurice and the Crisis of Christian Authority*, Oxford: OUP, 2005, pp. 85–6.

location of the apostolicity of the ministry within it, and reconnecting the authority of the ministry with that of the whole people of God.

Such a narrative can tell us much about the evolution of the theological meaning of the episcopate, but not about its actual exercise of authority, nor about the half-concealed and rarely articulated operative norms through which this putative meaning was expressed (or, equally likely, distorted or denied). If we want to get at what 'episcopal leadership' in the Church of England in the last 200 years really involved, and how it changed, we need to look elsewhere.

The Changing Language of Leadership

One useful index of the complications involved can be found in the history of language. Using the *Times Digital Archive* (covering the years 1785–1985), the *17th–18th Century Burney Collection of Newspapers*, and the *19th Century British Library Newspapers*, it is possible to search for occurrences of the phrases 'episcopal leadership' and 'bishop's leadership'.

No citations appear at all in the seventeenth and eighteenth centuries; 6 in the nineteenth century, and 11 citations (in the Times) from 1968 on. Yet 'episcopal' on its own yields over 18,000 citations in the *Times* alone, and on 'leadership' 4,750 citations before 1900. Instead, the word most used in connection with 'episcopal' or 'bishop's' was probably 'rule', which yields 195 nineteenth-century citations and 8 more in the twentieth (the latest in 1938). These figures perhaps do not sound all that impressive, but they are a far cry from the near-silence on 'leadership'. But note that the *17th–18th Century Burney Collection of Newspapers* yields no citations at all for 'episcopal rule' and 'bishop's rule' between 1600 and 1800.

This admittedly crude yardstick suggests at least an outline trajectory. The term 'leadership', as coupled with 'episcopal' and 'bishop', is largely a late-twentieth century usage. It was hardly used at all in the nineteenth century, and never before then. Instead, in the nineteenth century the much more common term was 'rule', not as a 'survival' from some pre-modern idea of hierarchy and divine right, but essentially as a nineteenth-century innovation.

The rise of the language of 'rule' might have been influenced by Tractarian or High Church conceptions of the threefold office of Christ and of the ministry, a renewed emphasis on the intrinsic spiritual authority of the episcopate, or a renewed confidence in the episcopal office as one of civic influence and governance. It was not a 'throwback' engineered by the alleged social conservatism of the Tractarians and others;[5] after all, many of the same bishops content to use the language of 'ruler' and 'rule' were pioneers of representative church government and of the voice of the laity in church affairs. George Ridding, for example, was almost certainly one of the few pre-1914 bishops to adopt the use of the wider and more 'democratic' baptismal franchise for the Southwell Diocesan Conference – wider, that is, than the more restricted (but much more common) communicants' franchise.[6] 'Rule' evidently did not connote autocracy, but rather responsible administration, albeit with a paternalistic face. That, perhaps, is a pointer to its decline in the 1920s and 1930s.

'Leadership', on the other hand, is a characteristically contemporary ascription, rarely found before the 1960s, which just happened to be the decade in which churchgoing underwent a sharp, steep contraction.[7] But why did 'leadership' come to be such a useful term, and such a problematic concept at the same time?

---

5 Simon Skinner, in *The Tractarians and the 'Condition of England*, Oxford: OUP, 2004, qualifies the over-simplistic view of Tractarianism as reactionary.

6 J.N. Morris, 'George Ridding and the Diocese of Southwell: A Study in the National Church Ideal', in *The Journal of Ecclesiastical History*, 61 (2010), pp. 125–42: p. 140.

7 Callum G. Brown, *The Death of Christian Britain: Understanding Secularisation 1800–2000*, London: Routledge, 2001; Hugh McLeod, *The Religious Crisis of the 1960s*, Oxford: OUP, 2007; Nigel Yates, *Love Now, Pay Later? Sex and Religion in the Fifties and Sixties*, London: SPCK, 2010. But note F.R. Barry's *Church and Leadership*, London: SCM, 1945.

The Early Nineteenth Century

Early nineteenth-century episcopacy (as for the preceding century and a half) assumed an intimate relationship to the court and to Westminster, and to the social rhythms of the elites who constituted the 'political nation' in the pre-Reform era.

Most bishops were aristocrats or gentry, with significant private income. This was, however, a relatively recent development. No less than 18 of the 73 bishops who held office at some point under Charles II, for example, had been of 'plebeian' origin, compared with only five from the nobility.[8] By the second half of George III's reign the proportion was reversed, with just one out of 32 who served between 1790 and 1820 coming from plebeian origins, compared with nine from the nobility. Of course, it was consistently true that the majority of bishops were from gentry or, broadly, 'genteel' backgrounds; nevertheless the virtual disappearance of humble origins, and the growing prominence of aristocratic origins, is very striking.[9]

Why had this change taken place? Whatever else they were – or rather, whatever functions they possessed as defined by canon law, ordinal and historic convention – bishops were a crucial element of the governance of pre-Reform (that is, pre-1832) Britain. But in the turbulent years of the sixteenth and seventeenth centuries, nobles in general terms sought other means than the Church for exercising power and influence, and the usefulness of bishops as servants of the Crown was underscored by the prominence of able but humble clergy who, through the grammar schools and Oxbridge, were able to acquire an education appropriate to their role. By the middle of the eighteenth century in two respects the ministry in general, and the episcopate in particular, had become of greater interest once

---

8 N. Ravitch, 'The Social Origins of French and English Bishops in the Eighteenth Century', *Historical Journal*, 8 (1965), pp. 309–25: p. 319.

9 Ravitch, 'Social Origins', p. 319.

again to the nobility and wealthy gentry. First, in an economy marked by a steady rise in agricultural income the attractiveness of church livings (dependent as they were particularly on income from glebe and from tithe) as a rich field of patronage was markedly increased. But along with this, the emergence of cabinet government in the eighteenth century, and especially under the long premiership of Robert Walpole, underlined the usefulness of the bishops to successive ministries.

Appointment to the episcopate became exceptionally vulnerable to external or non-ecclesiastical influences. As the historian William Gibson has pointed out, in practice the eighteenth and early nineteenth century were subject to an almost unprecedented degree of lay influence: '[f]rom patronage of a living to nomination to a see, laity dominated the Church'.[10] The widespread and mostly acceptable operation of clientage and patronage saw some – by our standards – unusual routes through to the episcopate. Thomas Burgess, for instance, was appointed to the see of St David by Prime Minister Addington, 'with whom he had been to school, but from whom he had not heard for almost 30 years.'[11] Burgess had only once been to Wales in his life.[12]

Examples such as this indicate why a later generation of Evangelicals and Tractarians could depict the pre-Reform bishops as worldly, Whiggish and craven, but there is plenty of evidence to suggest the Anglican episcopate pre-Reform was marked by significant examples of zealous, devout, reforming pastors, such as Burgess himself; whatever we think of the social world in which they lived, it did not prevent the emergence of able and energetic church leadership. Posterity has cast the bishops who voted against the Great Reform Bill in 1831 as 'out of touch', but arguably their resistance to reform

10 William T. Gibson, 'The Professionalization of an Elite: the Nineteenth Century Episcopate', *Albion*, 23 (1991), pp. 459–82: p. 460.

11 Gibson, 'Professionalization', p. 468.

12 'Thomas Burgess', *Oxford Dictionary of National Biography.*

merely expressed the perfectly rational response of those whose conception of pastoral care included a significant element of moral censure and social order. The bishops, whatever their social origins, were not simply obtuse or selfish defenders of the status quo, but in all likelihood profoundly believed that the Anglican settlement was intrinsic to domestic peace and human flourishing. For them, episcopal leadership essentially involved the competent management of routine episcopal duties, the conscientious exercise of patronage and political influence, and evident loyalty to the monarchy and the constitutional settlement. This was precisely why Radical critics of the established Church in the early nineteenth century invariably were so hostile to the bishops in particular.[13]

Nineteenth-Century Transitions

By the mid-nineteenth century, the social and political world of the episcopate was being transformed by a variety of different pressures, driven not least by rapid economic and social change. The most momentous was the programme of Church reform initiated by the State in the wake of the Reform crisis, and yet anticipated and also accompanied by the programme of diocesan reform so well delineated by Arthur Burns.[14] The Victorian clergy were dynamic change-makers who engineered an extraordinary revival in the fortunes of the Church of England. What we find in the middle of the nineteenth century is the emergence of a much more elevated, active and ultimately interventionist understanding of episcopal leadership. Reform of diocesan geography presupposed bishops who sought actively to control and manage their dioceses in person. Diocesan administration was rationalised and extended through

13 For a subtle re-reading of the myth of the 'Greek-play bishop' as a Radical satire which has passed into the historical conventions, see R.A. Burns and C. Stray, 'The Greek-play Bishop: Polemic, Prosopography, and Nineteenth-century Prelates', *Historical Journal*, 54 (2011), pp. 1013–1038.

14 Arthur R. Burns, *Diocesan Revival in the Church of England c.1800–1870*, Oxford: OUP, 1999.

the revival of the office of rural dean, the equalisation of see income, and the removal or diminution of interests (cathedral chapters, prebends, collegiate churches, non-resident clergy, lay patronage and sale of advowsons) which had previously acted as a check on the exercise of episcopal power.

The crucial turning-point was the sequence of parliamentary acts which preluded church reform and transformed the Church of England from a sole partner of the State (at least in England, Wales and Ireland) into one amongst a number of denominations, albeit one still in an unusually close relationship to the State. The abolition of discriminatory legislation against Dissenters and Roman Catholics in 1828–9, which enabled their formal entry into Parliament and ended any pretence that Parliament could act as the 'lay synod' of the Church of England, the Reform Act of 1832, the Irish Church Temporalities Act of 1833, the Municipal Reform Act of 1834, and the Marriage and Registration Acts of 1836 which established the civil registration of births, deaths and marriages, taken together, represented a constitutional revolution. Radical and Dissenting pressure for Disestablishment was given a fillip, and moved seriously onto the political agenda, being achieved in Ireland in 1869 and eventually in Wales in 1912 (enacted 1920), but never finally in England.

The dismantling of key elements of the 'confessional State' largely ended the significance of the bishops as constitutional and court leaders, and ushered in a period of intense internal division in the Church of England, not least because of the fierce criticism unleashed by the Tractarian movement in opposition to Whig/Liberal reform of the Church and in favour of a stronger concept of the Church's intrinsic spiritual authority and autonomy.

In this context, reform of the Church of England had a paradoxical effect. The State 'interference' bewailed by Newman, Keble *Changing Models of Episcopacy* and others, appeared to highlight the fragility of the Church, so that their clarion call to arms could be interpreted as a sign of a fearfulness that the Church was on the verge of being lost to hostile secular forces.[15] But in fact its purpose, as well as its effect, was unquestionably to strengthen the Church, removing obvious abuses, renewing its power of independent action, and enhancing its historic disciplinary and regulatory mechanisms.[16]

Lay patronage was a particularly significant index of changing sensibilities. Of the 10,693 benefices in England and Wales in 1821, some 6,619 were in the hands of private patrons, and just 1,301 in the hands of the bishops.[17] Running criticism of the patronage system concentrated mostly on the abuse of patronage sale, and not on the principle of private patronage *per se*, for private patronage – whether in the hands of individuals, or of trusts or corporate bodies such as colleges – was too useful a mechanism for placing family members in suitable livings (a phenomenon particularly true of the early part of the century), or for ensuring that clergymen of the 'right' doctrinal persuasion were placed in parishes (as with, for example, the operation of the Evangelical Simeon Trust), to be abandoned altogether. However it was also a particularly useful tool for ensuring episcopal control of benefices, and especially of newly-created benefices in urban areas. Accordingly, by the end of the century, even before the impact of major reform of patronage (ending sale) in 1898, episcopal patronage had more than doubled.[18] Church reform enhanced the power of diocesan bishops, and ultimately began to curtail the influence of lay patrons.

And yet the authority of the diocesan bishops in the nineteenth century did not rest solely on the reform of ecclesiastical machinery, but in some measure on their social prestige, and on the paternalism that flowed through social relations in this period.[19] The bishop, unconsciously or not, accrued to himself an assumption of social

15 J.H. Newman, *Thoughts on the Ministerial Commission, respectfully addressed to the clergy*, Oxford: Rivington, 1833.

16 See Frances Knight, *The Nineteenth-Century Church and English Society*, Cambridge: CUP, 1995.

17 M.J.D. Roberts, 'Private Patronage and the Church of England, 1800–1900', *Journal of Ecclesiastical History*, 32 (1981), pp. 199–223: p. 202.

18 Roberts, 'Private Patronage', loc. cit.

19 W. Bagehot, *The English Constitution*, London: Chapman & Hall, 1867, pp. 6–8.

influence which more than compensated for any post-1832 loss of income and actual political power. This was the period in which the language of 'rule' came to the fore. Bishops were municipal and civic leaders, and their local prominence depended in no small measure on their office, rather than on their birth and 'gentlemanly' qualities. Indeed it could even be argued that a certain 'professionalisation' was under way, with the establishment of a common route to episcopal preferment though the career trajectory of Oxbridge Fellow to headmaster of a public school to bishop. The prevailing assumption here was presumably that a combination of proven intellectual ability and administrative competence was not a function of birth and background, so much as of experience in running corporate bodies, and especially educational ones.

Bishops were still also commonly regarded as national intellectual leaders, a phenomenon probably on the wane by the early twentieth century, though masked by the prominence of men such as Charles Gore and William Temple. According to Gibson, almost a third of the nineteenth-century episcopate was drawn from men whose first posts after ordination were either a college fellowship or a teaching position.[20] That figure would rise significantly if subsequent posts before episcopal appointment were taken into account.

Reform and its effects cemented the episcopate's involvement in local and county affairs. Particularly in the mid and late-nineteenth century, before the construction of the welfare State, the prominence of philanthropy and the ideology of voluntarism ensured that churches were actively engaged in large-scale and widespread programmes designed to ameliorate homelessness, ill health, destitution and lack of education. The patronage and leadership ('rule') of the bishop were objects much sought after by Anglican charities, as well as by parishes promoting 'church extension' (the contemporary term for building new churches and creating new parishes). That is why the location of the cathedral in the newly

20 Gibson, 'Professionalization', p. 469.

created sees was often a source of much debate, with a strong current of opinion in favour of choosing the county town.[21] It is also the reason why episcopal appointment continued to be a prized aspect of Crown and prime-ministerial patronage, even as the bishops' political usefulness to particular administrations began to decline with political reform and the widening parliamentary franchise.[22] The list of qualities Gladstone desired in a bishop is testimony to the importance of the work he considered they had to perform: they included

> piety, learning, eloquence, administrative strength, energy, tact, allegiance to the Church, equitable spirit, knowledge of the world, accomplishment, ability to work with other bishops, legal understanding, circumspection, courage, maturity, and [significantly] 'Liberal' sentiments.[23]

Some historians have used the term 'professionalisation' to describe changes in the ordained ministry in the nineteenth century, pointing to the foundation of the new theological colleges and the reform of theological education, to the reform of the administration of clerical discipline, and to new and distinct concepts of pastoral work as exemplified in the increasing number of manuals devoted to parish and pastoral work.[24] One has to be sceptical about how far this can be pushed. 'Professionalisation' is a wonderfully plastic term that can be applied to developments in the ministry in almost any period. Definite changes did take place in the nineteenth century in the

21 P.S. Morrish, 'County and Urban Dioceses: Nineteenth-century Discussion on Ecclesiastical Geography', *Journal of Ecclesiastical History*, 26 (1975), pp. 279–300; and 'Parish-church Cathedrals, 1836–1931: Some Problems and their Solutions', *Journal of Ecclesiastical History,* 49 (1998), pp. 434–64.

22 See Nigel Scotland, 'Good and Proper Men': *Lord Palmerston and the Bench of Bishops*, Cambridge: James Clarke, 2000; William T. Gibson, 'Disraeli's Church Patronage', *Anglican and Episcopal History* 61 (1992), pp. 197–210, and '"A Great Excitement"; Gladstone and Church Patronage 1868–1890', in J. Loades (ed.), *Gladstone*, Bangor: Headstart, 1994.

23 Gibson, 'Professionalisation', p. 478, citing his own article, '"A Great Excitement"'.

24 Cf. the discussion in Anthony Russell, *The Clerical Profession*, London: SPCK, 1980; also, Rosemary O'Day, 'The Men from the Ministry', in Gerald Parsons (ed.), *Religion in Victorian Britain*, vol. 2: *Controversies*, Manchester: Open University, 1988, pp. 258–79.

assumptions underpinning the measurement of episcopal suitability, however. By the mid-nineteenth century, the gradual dismantling of the system of clientage and patronage which had underpinned the operation not only of the Church, but also of the armed forces and the law, now meant clergy who were ambitious were encouraged to work hard to prove themselves.

By the end of the century, the epitome of the diocesan bishop was a figure such as the relentlessly energetic George Ridding. Ridding showed an active concern in practically every possible aspect of his diocese's church life. 'Church work', he said, 'is the spread of temperance, and purity, and honesty, and kindness. I should like to know the agencies in each parish, to promote mental, moral and social advance.'[25] He spent much of his own considerable private fortune on church extension in the new diocese of Southwell, and patronised charitable agencies across Nottinghamshire. According to his wife, he was proud of his attempts to intervene in industrial disputes in the county, including the great coal lockout of 1893, the 'Coal War'.[26] This was a far cry from the courtly, noble bishops of the previous century.

Twentieth Century

The rise of the Labour movement, reform of local government and welfare, above all the democratisation of parliamentary government – all this in time forced a dramatic change in the scope of a bishop's authority and in the degree of influence he could exercise. It was precisely because of his realisation that the arrival of mass democracy required the Church to transform its governance that William Temple, the leading figure in the reform-minded 'Life and Liberty' movement during the First World War, pressed for the Church of

25 George Ridding, *The Church and Commonwealth: The Visitation Charges*, London: Edward Arnold, 1906, p. 14.

26 Laura Ridding, *George Ridding, Schoolmaster and Bishop*, London: Edward Arnold, 1908, pp. 265–8.

England to adopt a baptismal franchise (i.e. the widest possible franchise compatible with professed Trinitarian belief) for the new system of church governance formalised by the Enabling Act of 1919, in preference to the confirmation franchise urged by Anglo-Catholics. The Church Assembly subsequently created in fact never fulfilled Temple's hope for mass working-class participation in the Church of England. Nevertheless, even as they seemingly endorsed the principles of the new mass democracy within the Church itself, in a wider sphere the bishops were gradually losing significant political influence. This was perhaps acutely symbolised by the failure of the Prayer Book revision proposals in Parliament in 1927 and 1928, coming as it did in the wake of almost a generation's hard work developing and refining liturgical revision.

Much has been made – rightly – of the continuing power of Christianity between the wars to shape and articulate the aspirations and identities of the nation.[27] This is particularly evident in the concept of 'Christian civilisation' which was to help express growing distaste for fascism, and especially Nazism, up to and into the Second World War, and which featured so tellingly in Churchill's wartime speeches. This persisting influence – characterised by Callum Brown as the 'salvation economy' – can be traced even in the new suburbs of London, where churchgoing remained a significant feature of local life.[28] It co-existed, however, with troubling evidence of a gradual decline in active church membership in most of the mainstream denominations, including Anglicanism.[29] And it also helped to conceal a certain diminution of the social and political standing of the bishops. Nothing illustrates this better, perhaps, than the mostly ill-fated efforts of bishops to intervene in industrial disputes. Famously, Bishop Westcott had 'broken the impasse' in the Durham

---

27 Cf. Matthew Grimley, *Citizenship, Community, and the Church of England: Liberal Anglican Theories of the State between the Wars*, Oxford: OUP, 2004.

28 Rex A. Walford, *The Growth of 'New London' in Suburban Middlesex (1918–1945) and the Response of the Church of England*, New York: Edwin Mellen, 2007.

29 Clive D. Field, 'Gradualist or Revolutionary Secularization? A Case Study of Religious Belonging in Inter-War Britain 1918–1939', *Church History and Religious Culture*, 93 (2013), pp. 57–93.

miners' strike of 1892 by inviting both sides to his house – an incident commemorated in the stained glass of All Saints' Church, next to Westcott House in Cambridge.[30] The efforts of William Temple – then Bishop of Manchester – and others to mediate in the General Strike in 1926 were controversial and came to nothing. But even more tellingly, the previous year, during the national coalminers' dispute that led up to the General Strike, the Durham miners, mistaking the Dean of Durham, James Welldon, for the Bishop, Hensley Henson, nearly threw him into the River Wear.[31] Above all, it was perhaps the perceived role of Archbishop Lang in the abdication crisis of 1936 that ended for a couple of generations the capacity of bishops to intervene decisively in national affairs.[32]

Notwithstanding their gradual marginalisation from social and political life (and it was gradual, and by no means smooth), the bishops remained, like most political leaders (bar the new Labour Party) predominantly a private school and Oxbridge-educated elite well into the mid- or even late-twentieth century. Yet it is important to emphasise that a shared social background and education did not necessarily produce passivity or obsequiousness in the face of the State. Early and mid-twentieth century bishops viewed themselves as leaders of Christian conscience.[33] As Andrew Chandler notes:

> However influenced by the attitudes of their social class the bishops may have been, and however many landed connections they might enjoy, they remained conscious that as Christians they must justify themselves by principle, at every turn, and not by the opportunity of the moment or the advantage of party.[34]

---

30. Owen Chadwick, *The Victorian Church, Part Two: 1860–1901*, 2nd edn, London: SCM, 1872, p. 285.

31. Owen Chadwick, *Hensley Henson: A Study in the Friction between Church and State*, 2nd edn, Norwich: Canterbury Press, 1994, pp. 166-7.

32 Cf. Robert Beaken, *Cosmo Lang. Archbishop in War and Crisis*, London: Tauris, 2012.

33 Grimley, *Citizenship*; A. Chandler, 'The Church of England and the Obliteration Bombing of Germany in the Second World War', *English Historical Review,* 108 (1993), pp. 920–46.

34 Chandler, 'Church of England', p. 923.

The sociologist David Morgan suggests that a shift took place in the course of the twentieth century, which took bishops out of the world of deference and patrician responsibility described above.[35] Instead,

> we see the growth of the 'professional' bishop, required to spend much time in diocesan administration, sitting on committees and participating in commissions, attentive to the concerns of the Church and her mission rather than to any external considerations.[36]

Of course, the change was far from absolute. George Ridding, for example, was definitely a 'professional' bishop, and yet he died in 1904. And some bishops continued to operate along 'older' lines even as the world around them was changing. A surprising example, perhaps, was George Bell (1883–1958; Bishop of Chichester 1929–58) who, for all his upbringing in the reign of Victoria, is more conventionally considered in the light of his ecumenical commitments, his friendship with Dietrich Bonhoeffer and his opposition to saturation bombing, all causes which have tended to position him as one of the most prominent of 'modern' bishops in the twentieth-century Church of England. Chandler has claimed that Bell's humanitarian interests to some extent put him at odds with the 'growing tendency [of bishops] in the church to concentrate primarily on its own affairs and to organise its structures more efficiently.'[37] Yet Bell's characteristic habits of mind, and his modes of administration, were typically those of the late-nineteenth and early twentieth century.

Also changing were the social background and status of the bishops and of other senior clergy.[38] The falling attractiveness of the Church

---

35 D.H.J. Morgan, 'The Social and Educational Background of Anglican Bishops – Continuities and Changes', *The British Journal of Sociology*, 20 (1969), pp. 295–310.

36 Morgan, 'Social and Educational Background', p. 308.

37 'George Bell', *Oxford Dictionary of National Biography.*

38 Robert Towler and Anthony P.M. Coxon, *The Fate of the Anglican Clergy*, London: Macmillan, 1979; Russell, *The Clerical Profession.*

as a horizon of ambition for the gentry and aristocracy accompanied accelerating educational opportunities for the lower middle and working classes from mid-century. Whereas some 33% of the bench were sons of aristocracy and gentry in 1860, this figure had fallen to just 2% by 1960; by contrast, the proportion of those with professional fathers had risen from 61% in 1860 to 70% a hundred years later, with the increase in sons of clergy particularly noticeable, from 18% to 54%.[39] Even in 1960, however, Morgan could find no bishop whose father could definitely be described as a manual worker.[40] His conclusion bears quotation here:

> Speaking generally, we may characterise the change in the backgrounds of bishops as depicting a shift from a situation where the episcopacy was part of a broader social elite to one where it is a more narrowly defined ecclesiastical elite.[41]

In the 1860s, according to Morgan, six bishops had been educated at Eton; by 1960, just one had been.[42] The trend Morgan described has not been reflected in ongoing change, arguably, though statistics about social background are not easy to come by. In 2014, in the wake of the appointment of Justin Welby as Archbishop of Canterbury, the *Church Times* carried out a brief survey of the educational background of the bench of bishops, finding that nearly 50% had been educated privately, with just 13% having attended a comprehensive school.[43] Nevertheless, even this was a noteworthy shift away from the situation a hundred years earlier.

Arguably our anxieties today about episcopal leadership echo this shift. For all that it often feels as if the Church of England continues to function largely as a traditional, hierarchical institution, conservative in outlook and led mostly by people drawn from a

---

39 Morgan, 'Social and Educational Background', p. 297.

40 Morgan, 'Social and Educational Background', p. 298.

41 Morgan, 'Social and Educational Background', p. 299.

42 Morgan, 'Social and Educational Background', p. 299.

43 *Church Times*, 5 September 2014.

relatively small social and educational elite, in fact anyone occupying a position of responsibility in the Church, whether lay or ordained, whether senior or junior, has to operate in a context in which authority is being constantly challenged and therefore constantly negotiated.

It is no longer easy to assume that bishops are significant shapers of public opinion; their views carry some weight, it is true, as far as one can judge from media attention, but at the same time they are just one source of opinion amongst a bewildering variety of voices. Until the rapid cultural changes that began in the 1960s and 1970s, bishops were generally considered to be amongst the foremost guardians of public morality (hence the outrage at John Robinson's stance in the *Lady Chatterley* trial), but that is no longer the case – and after all, what is 'public morality' today? What bishops are able to say with authority, and especially the question of who will listen to them with sympathy when they do speak out, has been immensely complicated by the inexorable rise of the 'rights' agenda. If the arguments over gay marriage show anything, it is the near impossibility nowadays of the Church of England shaping public opinion (or should I say 'resisting' the tide of public opinion) on a question widely perceived to be one of equality before the law. Furthermore, if bishops are no longer the authoritative public figures that they once were, neither are they perceived to be authoritative teachers of religious truth: the transformation in the life of universities since the Robbins report, and the rise of religious studies and 'secular' theology departments, have significantly shifted the focus of critical, constructive theology away from ecclesial preoccupations.

Conclusion

What this paper has sought to demonstrate is that close study of the history of the episcopate not only helps us to see the evolution of its exercise of authority through several perceptible stages over the last two hundred years, but also the pervasive influence of a vast range (and this piece has no more than scratched the surface) of factors that have arisen from the embedding of the institutions of the Church in the social history of the nation. Bishops may have lost much of the social prestige which once sustained their practical exercise of authority, just as the intricate patterns of social relationship which constituted British society have mutated and diversified bewilderingly over the last two centuries, but their task of pastoring, encouraging and challenging the Christian community continues to be shaped, as it always was, by a delicate fusion of traditional, liturgical, Scriptural and yet also social and political norms.

All in all, the evolution of episcopal leadership in the modern Church of England has been the result of a complex matrix of factors which include many things hidden from the usual theological discussion, not least as they bear on the social, political and economic conditions in which episcopacy has to be exercised. If this points to anything concrete, it is the sheer complexity and diversity demanded of senior clergy by the world in which we live. A single or preferred model of episcopal leadership is unlikely to gain much traction.

2.5 Evangelical Models of Leadership: General Trends and Anglican Expressions

David Hilborn

In his influential book *Ministry in Three Dimensions*, Steven Croft notes that among evangelical churches, ministers and parachurch agencies the term 'leader' is becoming 'the most commonly-used title for a person called to full-time Christian work'. He goes on to chart manifestations of this trend in conferences and courses which are routinely advertised for 'leaders', in mission organisations' promotion of 'leadership' training, and in an increasing stream of publications focused on the beliefs, attitudes, skills and techniques required to be an effective 'leader'.[1] Croft's study is particularly focused on the English Anglican context – he is now Bishop of Sheffield, having previously served as Warden of Cranmer Hall, Durham, and as a vicar in Halifax. This denominational perspective is reflected more especially in his concern for how such generic leadership language might impact the traditional understanding of public ministry encoded in the formularies of the Church of England:

> This change of use in the way we describe the ordained should give us pause for thought. There is a danger of a gap opening up between a popular understanding of what ordination is about ('leadership') and the Church's understanding of that ministry captured in its liturgy and especially in the ordinals, which do

1 Steven Croft, *Ministry in Three Dimensions: Ordination and Leadership in the Local Church*, new edn, London: Darton, Longman & Todd, 2008, p. 25.

> not use the word. There is a deeper danger of the Church as a whole beginning to use a word to describe the work.[2]

As Croft acknowledges, another Anglican writer, John Finney, highlights this danger in his earlier study *Understanding Leadership* (1989). Surveying the New Testament, Finney suggests that the key terms that should inform a Christian approach to leadership are Servant, Shepherd, Steward and *Episkopos*.[3] Nowhere, however, does it appear that those responsible for ministry in the New Testament church are referred to by the most common Greek word for leaders in the civic and commercial life of the ancient Near-East – *archon*. As Croft remarks, this church

> clearly thought very deeply about the different titles used to describe those charged with different responsibilities among the people of God ... and was deliberately shy of leadership language and titles taken from the society of the day. Surely, there is a lesson for the contemporary Church.

Croft goes on to suggest that while English Anglican Evangelicals have still sought to ground generic leadership discourses 'at least superficially' in the biblical tradition, other parts of the Church of England have absorbed them 'as it were, undiluted and unrooted in Scripture'.[4]

In this paper I want to show that while Croft's analysis may be broadly true for Evangelicals in the Church of England, Evangelicalism as a whole has been far more prone to take its cues from generic leadership, management, and organisational paradigms. Moreover, I will suggest that as these paradigms become more pervasive, they are likely to challenge English Anglican Evangelicals, as well as others, to think more deeply and more critically about the meaning of 'leadership' and its application in the Christian context.

---

2 Croft, *Ministry*, p. 26.

3 John Finney, *Understanding Leadership*, London: Daybreak, 1989, pp. 43–69.

4 Croft, *Ministry*, p. 26.

Defining 'Evangelicalism'

Definitions of Evangelicalism in general and of Anglican Evangelicalism in particular are highly contested. Historically, debates about the term 'Evangelicalism' tend to focus on the relative importance of the Reformation and the British and American revivals of the mid-eighteenth century for its origination.[5] This in turn is linked to tensions between the characteristic use of the term 'Evangelical' as a synonym for 'Protestant' on the European continent (e.g. in the German *evangelisch*), and its deployment in a more particularly revivalist-pietistic sense in the UK, the USA and elsewhere.[6] Theologically, there is disagreement about the extent to which Evangelicalism should be defined in its essence as a conservative form of orthodox, creedal Christianity, and the extent to which it can be identified in relation to more distinctive doctrines such as biblical inerrancy, penal substitutionary atonement, new birth and creationism.[7] Methodologically, there is argument about the degree to which Evangelicalism may be delineated by a distinctive approach to mission and evangelism.[8] Ecclesiologically and culturally, there is dispute about whether or not Pentecostals should be classed as Evangelicals.[9]

Within Anglicanism, disagreements periodically arise over these wider issues, but more specific intra-denominational debate concerns

---

5 See Michael A.G. Haykin and Kenneth J. Stewart (eds), *The Emergence of Evangelicalism: Exploring Historical Continuities*, Leicester: Apollos, 2008.

6 R.V.P., in W.A. Elwell, *Evangelical Dictionary of Theology*, Grand Rapids, MI: Baker Academic, 2001, pp. 405–410.

7 See e.g. Geoffrey W. Grogan, *The Faith Once Entrusted to the Saints? Engaging with Issues and Trends in Evangelical Theology*, Leicester: IVP, 2010; Gregory A. Boyd and Paul R. Eddy, *Across the Spectrum: Understanding Issues in Evangelical Theology*, Grand Rapids, MI: Baker Academic, 2002.

8 Bill J. Leonard, 'Evangelism and Contemporary American Life', in Paul W. Chilcote and Layceye C. Warner (eds), *The Study of Evangelism: Exploring a Missional Practice of the Church*, Grand Rapids, MI: Eerdmans, 2008, pp. 101–16.

9 Amos Yong, *The Spirit Poured Out on All Flesh: Pentecostalism and the Possibility of a Global Theology*, Grand Rapids: Baker Academic, 2005, pp. 21, 32.

whether 'Anglican' should function as a qualifier of the root identifier 'Evangelical', or vice-versa – i.e. whether one is first and foremost an Evangelical who happens to express Evangelicalism in an Anglican context, or whether one is primarily an Anglican who expresses Anglicanism in its evangelical form.[10]

While acknowledging these definitional problems, for the purposes of this paper I shall use a model based on the landmark historical work of David Bebbington – one which does not attempt a comprehensive or prescriptive anatomy of all that Evangelicals hold in common with other classical Christian traditions, but which instead seeks to identify those key emphases which make Evangelicalism distinctive as compared with other forms of Christianity. This model highlights four key characteristics:

- **Conversionism** – The belief that lives must be changed through repentance and personal faith in Christ, often arrived at through a 'crisis' experience.
- **Activism** – The expression of the gospel in effort, as demonstrated in evangelism and social service.
- **Biblicism** – A particular regard for the Bible, lived out devotionally and defined doctrinally in terms of the 'supreme', 'primary' or 'inerrant' authority of Scripture.
- **Crucicentrism** – A characteristic stress on the cross of Christ as central for understanding divine atonement and salvation. [11]

From time to time critiques of Bebbington's quadrilateral are suggested by scholars of Evangelicalism. Yet the leading American evangelical historian, Mark Noll, speaks for most when he identifies

10 Compare, for example, Melvin Tinker (ed.), *The Anglican Evangelical Crisis, Fearn: Christian Focus,* 1995 with R.T. France and Alister E. McGrath, *Evangelical Anglicans: Their Role and Influence in the Church Today,* London: SPCK, 1993.

11 David W. Bebbington, *Evangelicalism in Modern Britain: a History from the 1730s to the 1980s*, London: Unwin & Hyman, 1989, pp. 2–19.

it as 'the most serviceable general definition' available.[12] For our purposes it is significant that the least contentious corner of the grid is probably the second: indeed, I would propose that the characteristic activism and pragmatism of Evangelicals makes them especially amenable to 'leadership' paradigms drawn from beyond the Church and, more importantly, to the importation of those paradigms without the level of Scriptural and doctrinal scrutiny one might otherwise expect from a tradition identified with 'biblicism'. Croft may be right that Evangelicals within the Church of England are *relatively* more circumspect about generic 'leadership' discourse than certain others within the denomination, but insofar as they see themselves as Evangelicals first and Anglicans second, and insofar as Evangelicalism as a whole will be shown here to lead the way in absorbing such models, this relative claim may not actually amount to much in the way of mitigation.

Evangelical Activism and Pragmatism as Amenable to Generic 'Leadership' Approaches

Both in his 1974 D. Phil. thesis 'The Pan-Evangelical Impulse in Britain 1798–1830', and in his subsequent book *Evangelicals United: Ecumenical Stirrings in Pre-Victorian Britain*,[13] Roger H. Martin focuses not on any great integration of evangelical theology or ecclesiology in the period specified, but rather, on a surge of united evangelical action. Specifically, he applies the adjective 'pan-evangelical' to groups like the London Missionary Society, the Religious Tract Society, the British and Foreign Bible Society, and the London City Mission – groups whose formation from 1795

12 Mark A. Noll, *American Evangelical Christianity: An Introduction*, Oxford: Blackwell, 2001, p. 185. For an alternative definition and discussion of Bebbington's model see Timothy Larsen, 'Defining and Locating Evangelicalism', in Timothy Larsen and Daniel J. Treier (eds), *The Cambridge Companion to Evangelical Theology*, Cambridge: Cambridge University Press, 2007, pp. 1–14.

13 Roger H. Martin, '*The Pan-Evangelical impulse in Britain, 1798–1830*', D.Phil. thesis, University of Oxford, 1974; *Evangelicals United: Ecumenical Stirrings in Pre-Victorian Britain 1795–1830*, Metuchen, NJ / London: Scarecrow Press, 1983.

onwards heralded a new era of collaboration between Anglicans and Nonconformists, independents and connexionalists, Arminians and Calvinists. Like Martin, Doreen Rosman has pointed out that the rise of the great pan-evangelical mission societies and para-church agencies through the nineteenth century 'proved to be essentially pragmatic'. As she puts it, they 'sought and acquired influential patronage, mobilised mass support by constructing a network of local auxiliaries, and co-operated with any who shared their aims *regardless of belief*.'[14] Or as Kenneth Hylson-Smith observes, with specific reference to the British and Foreign Bible Society, it 'was viewed as an essentially Christian business venture, with a single objective [to distribute the Bible], *which did not impinge on denominational interests or autonomy.*'[15]

A similar downplaying of specific denominational and ecclesiological affiliations was a feature of the socio-political activism that marked evangelical religion in the nineteenth century. The educational reformer Hannah More (1745–1843) was an Anglican, but her impressive social entrepreneurship and dedicated networking across ecclesiastical and parliamentary boundaries saw her labelled a 'Methodist' and a 'she-bishop'. Far more important than distinctive theologies of ministry or church polity, however, was her impulse to lead God's work in schooling the poor: in this as in other spheres, she wrote, 'action is the life of virtue, and the world is the theatre of action.'[16] The same drive to provide Christian leadership in society above and beyond specific 'faith and order' concerns was evident in the anti-slavery campaign advanced by William Wilberforce and others, and in the later factory reform acts steered through parliament by Anthony Ashley Cooper, the Seventh Earl of Shaftesbury.[17] It is noticeable that each of these great evangelical

---

14 Doreen Rosman, *Evangelicals and Culture*, London: Croom Helm, 1984, p. 23, my emphasis.

15 Kenneth Hylson-Smith, 'Roots of Pan-Evangelicalism: 1735–1835', in Steve Brady and Harold Rowdon (eds), *For Such a Time as This: Perspectives on Evangelicalism, Past, Present and Future*, Milton Keynes: Scripture Union / London: Evangelical Alliance, 1996, p. 144, my emphasis.

16 Hannah More, *An Estimate of the Religion of the Fashionable World*, London, 1808, p. 146.

17 Bebbington, *Evangelicalism*, p. 12.

figures was a layperson; indeed, as Bebbington recalls, for Evangelicals in the Church of Scotland, in Methodism and in various branches of Nonconformity, even more than in the Church of England at this time, the imperative of 'doing the gospel' conspicuously superseded formal clergy–lay distinctions. Indeed, as Evangelicals came together from different backgrounds to make common cause in evangelism and social action, so a positive virtue was made of combining ecclesiastical, civic and business leadership in interdenominational projects, societies and councils. For example, the Evangelical Alliance, founded in 1846, had drafted onto its Executive by 1880 six peers and seven MPs, the Lord Mayor of London and a High Court judge, alongside the Dean of Canterbury.[18]

This pan-evangelical pragmatism, and the generic leadership paradigms which accompanied it, waned somewhat during the first half of the twentieth century. During this period the rise and perceived dominance of liberal Protestantism prompted many Evangelicals to retrench to their parishes, pastorates, and denominations in what David Moberg has called 'the great reversal'.[19] However, the British Crusades led by the American evangelist Billy Graham in the 1950s and '60s, coupled with a newly-resurgent social concern provoked by the 'permissive society', global poverty, and disease, saw a recovery of pan-evangelical activism which continues to this day, and which is exemplified by a plethora of campaigning parachurch organisations including TEAR Fund, CARE for the Family, Christians in Parliament, the AIDS charity ACET, and many more.[20] Here again, as in the nineteenth century, the accent is on what the Canadian evangelical theologian John

18 Executive Council Minutes, Vol. III, 10 November 1880, p. 320.

19 David Moberg, *The Great Reversal: Evangelism versus Social Concern*, London: Scripture Union, 1973.

20 Tim Chester, *Awakening to a World of Need: Recovery of Evangelical Social Concern*, Leicester: IVP, 1993; Ian Randall and David Hilborn, *One Body in Christ: The History and Significance of the Evangelical Alliance*, Carlisle: Paternoster, 2001, pp. 208–82.

Stackhouse calls 'a spirit of pragmatic compromise.'[21] As Stackhouse puts it, the very nature of transdenominational Evangelicalism 'militates against elaborate theological sophistication and precision, as it seeks only the *minimal theological ground* on which to proclaim the gospel.' Precisely because it is concerned 'only for theological essentials in its drive to evangelise the world and foster spiritual vitality,' distinctions of, say, episcopal, presbyteral, diaconal, monastic, scholarly, evangelistic or preaching ministry in such contexts tend to be dissolved into less nuanced and less historically freighted concepts of 'leadership'.

In what follows we will examine six models of evangelical leadership that to varying degrees either arise from or seek to modify the context just described.

Key Models of 'Christian Leadership' Adopted by Anglican and Other Evangelicals

1. The Parachurch Entrepreneur

With hindsight, Billy Graham's post-war evangelistic campaigns can be seen as particularly important for the re-shaping of British evangelical approaches to leadership along the more generic lines set out above. Graham himself was ordained as a Southern Baptist minister in 1939, but from his first visit to the UK in 1946 with the parachurch agency Youth for Christ, he was identified as a trans-denominational 'leader' rather than a Baptist pastor. The key sponsor and organiser of his subsequent rallies here was the parachurch Evangelical Alliance rather than any particular church or church-based ecumenical body. Indeed, after encountering relative indifference from the Archbishop of Canterbury, Geoffrey Fisher, and from the British Council of Churches in 1952, the Alliance

21 John G. Stackhouse, 'More than a Hyphen: Twentieth Century Canadian Evangelicalism in Anglo-American Context', in George Rawlyk and Mark Noll (eds), *Amazing Grace: Evangelicalism in Australia, Britain, Canada and the United States*, Grand Rapids, MI: Baker, 1993, p. 394.

determined that any future campaign would best be brokered by 'a body of responsible enthusiasts outside ecclesiastical organisation'.[22] By this point, Graham had achieved remarkable success with expertly choreographed rallies that had seen prominent sporting and showbusiness celebrities converted, and had formed his own Billy Graham Evangelistic Association to carry forward this work. By 'professionalising' and 'entrepreneurialising' ministry in this way Graham was in one sense following in the footsteps of a succession of 'name-brand' itinerant American evangelists from the previous hundred years or more, including Charles Finney, Dwight L. Moody, and Billy Sunday. Yet his exportation of this model to the UK, and the remarkable success of his rallies at Harringay in 1954 and in the subsequent Greater London campaign of 1966, helped to embed here a trans-ecclesial form of 'Christian leadership' which would proliferate in the years that followed – both through the parachurch agencies mentioned above, but also, ironically, in more local church situations.

By the 1980s British evangelists and teachers like Arthur Wallis, Derek Prince, and Bob Gordon had established 'named' itinerant ministries, and new networks of Charismatic Evangelical and so-called Restorationist churches had grown under the leadership of 'apostolic' figures like Bryn Jones, Gerald Coates, Roger and Faith Forster and Colin Urquhart.[23] The Evangelical Alliance helped found the annual Spring Harvest festival, again centred on 'named' speakers, set-piece celebrations, and preaching events.[24] A highly successful Alliance-sponsored conference held at Prestatyn and called 'Leadership '84', epitomised many of the trends we have been identifying.[25] Not all of these phenomena owed a direct debt to the 'Billy Graham effect', but the general influence was plain.

---

22 Randall and Hilborn, *One Body*, p. 223.

23 Andrew Walker, *Restoring the Kingdom: The Radical Christianity of the House Church Movement*, revised edn, Guildford: Eagle, 1998.

24 Randall and Hilborn, *One Body*, pp. 283–308.

25 Randall and Hilborn, *One Body*, pp. 286–87.

Interestingly, not every Anglican Evangelical who attended Leadership '84 felt comfortable with the business and management-based models that were prominent there. Some also appear to have struggled with the dominant preference for extemporary charismatic worship over anything recognisably liturgical. It seems likely, however, that their discomfort stemmed not so much from pure ecclesiological conviction as from attachment to an older leadership model which was hardly less 'secular', but which was, perhaps, more congruent with the Church of England's identity as an established church. It is to this that we turn next.

2. The Patrician Influencer

In the analysis of distinctive evangelical leadership models we mentioned at the outset, Steven Croft observes that an older generation of clergy, now mostly retired or nearing retirement,

> were prepared for the exercise of leadership in the Christian Church not through their theological colleges but through their public schools, universities and national service and a related network of Christian camps and organisations.[26]

The network to which Croft refers included Pathfinders, the Young Churchmen's Fellowship and the Inter-School Christian Fellowship. In the Church of England context, however, one of the most significant manifestations of such 'establishment' formation was the programme of 'camps for public schoolboys' run by the Children's Special Service Mission (CSSM) from 1892.

CSSM camps were originally conceived and run by Anglican ordinands studying at Cambridge, but from 1924 they were re-titled 'Varsities and Public School Camps' and from 1932 were co-ordinated by a young clergyman called Eric Nash, affectionately known as 'Bash'. Thoroughly evangelical in ethos, these camps were

26 Croft, *Ministry*, p. 22.

to some extent designed as an antidote to the perceived dullness and nominalism of chapel religion in independent schools. Yet by targeting boys in so narrowly upper and upper middle class a sector of society they were also unashamedly elitist. As his biographer J. Edison records, Bash concentrated his efforts on the top 30 or so public schools for the simple reason that they contained a 'high proportion of the future leaders of the country.' Therefore, 'to reach them with the gospel opened the possibility of reaching future rulers, men with an immense influence over their contemporaries.'[27]

On their own terms, 'Bash Camps' were highly successful, shaping the lives and ministries of a whole generation of key evangelical leaders including John Stott, Michael Green, Dick Lucas, and David Watson.[28] Yet, for all the biblical teaching and discipleship training they offered, it is still noticeable that they operated with a relatively uncritical acceptance of secular hierarchy and power. In this sense, they are prone to similar hermeneutical criticism as might be levelled at unfiltered application of secular management, business, or civic paradigms of leadership.

3. The Intradenominational Networker

Whereas Christian camps such as those run by Nash were 'ancillary' to established denominational structures, another extra-parochial model of evangelical leadership entails active commitment to and involvement in the councils, committees, synods and assemblies of the church, the better to effect change and renewal 'from within'. This model is perhaps the most common among loyal evangelical Church of England clergy who seek to serve more than simply their own parish. Examples abound, but among those in this category of 'Intradenominational Networkers' who have written autobiographies

27 J. Edison (ed.), *Bash: A Study in Spiritual Power,* London: Marshall Pickering, 1982.

28 Pete Ward, *Growing Up Evangelical: Youthwork and the Making of a Subculture*, London: SPCK, 1996, pp. 36–41.

in recent years, Michael Saward (1932–2015) would be typical. In addition to incumbencies in Fulham and Ealing, his diverse and quintessentially activist evangelical career included serving as Secretary of Liverpool Council of Churches and Radio and Television Officer to Archbishop Michael Ramsey. Until retiring in 2000 he was Canon Treasurer of St Paul's Cathedral. Prior to that he was a member of the General Synod between 1975 and 1995, and served as Church Commissioner from 1978 to 1993 and a member of the Church of England Evangelical Council from 1976 to 1993.[29] Given this track record of avowedly ecclesiastical work, it is perhaps not surprising that Saward was passionate in encouraging Anglican Evangelicals to re-focus their attention from parachurch initiatives to Church as such – from pragmatic pan-evangelical endeavours grounded in minimalist statements of faith to authentic evangelical engagement with ecclesiology in general, and their own denominational ecclesiology in particular:

> By the mid-nineteenth century evangelicals in all or most of the post-Reformation churches felt a strong desire to find common ground and fellowship and did so by creating cross-denominational organisations with a doctrinal basis which stressed the Bible and the doctrine of justification by grace through faith. Matters concerning church, ministry, and sacraments were deliberately excluded ... but in the last forty years evangelicals in the Church of England have rediscovered their inheritance, re-acknowledged their ecclesiological foundation ... Thus the issue of ecclesiology, the doctrine of the church, is becoming increasingly important in the creation of a mind-set.[30]

Saward is alluding here to the pivotal Keele Congress of 1967, when Anglican Evangelicals overwhelmingly determined to recommit

29 Michael Saward, *A Faint Streak of Humility: An Autobiography,* Carlisle: Paternoster Press, 1999.

30 Michael Saward, 'At Root, It's a Matter of Theology', in Graham Cray et al., *The Post-Evangelical Debate*, London: Triangle, 1997, pp. 92–3.

themselves to involvement in the leadership and decision-making structures of the Church of England, rather than hunkering down in their localities or breaking away to form a new pan-evangelical network, as the Free Church preacher Martyn Lloyd Jones had suggested in debate with John Stott the year before.[31] Yet Keele was also about a commitment to leading in ecumenical affairs, and this relates to our next model.

4. The Ecumenist

As well as occupying leading roles within their own particular ecclesial context, Anglican Evangelicals may choose to express their commitment to the one, holy, catholic, and apostolic Church by taking a lead in ecumenical affairs. In doing so, they will either consciously or unconsciously mitigate the ambivalence and even the hostility felt by previous generations of Evangelicals towards the ecumenical movement.

The World Evangelical Alliance was reconstituted in 1951 as the World Evangelical Fellowship (WEF), partly in response to the founding of the World Council of Churches in 1948, but its initial stance towards WCC-style ecumenism was limited to 'benevolent neutrality' on the grounds that the WCC was defined too much by a liberal Protestant agenda. In 1974, however, the evangelical Lausanne Covenant offered an alternative approach through a fresh evangelical vision of mission based on both personal conversion and social transformation. Later, the WEF re-styled itself the 'World Evangelical Alliance', took on a fuller observational role at WCC assemblies, and participated in an extensive dialogue with the Roman Pontifical Council for Christian Unity (1993–2002).

While fundamentalists and certain more conservative evangelical bodies continue to make disavowal of the ecumenical movement an article of faith, the decline of liberal modernist influence and the

31 Randall and Hilborn, *One Body*, pp. 246–50.

growth of evangelical and Pentecostal churches since the 1980s has been a factor in prompting the WCC to shift from a relatively 'centripetal' model of visible institutional unity to a relatively 'centrifugal' or devolved paradigm. One major expression of this was the founding in 1998 of the Global Christian Forum, an informal network in which WCC members could interact with leaders of non-WCC affiliated bodies on matters of mutual concern. In this changed landscape, Evangelicals, and not least Anglican Evangelicals, have come to play a more prominent role. An example of such involvement would be Sarah Rowland Jones, an evangelical ordained in the Church in Wales who later served as Ecumenical Adviser to the Archbishop of Cape Town, as a member of the Inter-Anglican Standing Commission on Ecumenical Relations, and as an Executive Committee member of the GCF.[32]

5. The Church Growth Strategist

We have already shown how Billy Graham became a significant figure in the development of British parachurch models of evangelical leadership after the Second World War. Another significant connection between Graham and changing approaches to leadership in British Evangelicalism came through Fuller Theological Seminary in Pasdena, California. Founded in 1947, the seminary soon developed into one of the leading American evangelical centres for ministerial training and theological study. Billy Graham joined its Board in 1958, at a time when both he and the institution were looking to shed its original fundamentalist ethos, and he continued to be involved for many years afterwards.[33] In its turn, during the 1970s Fuller became the wellspring for a movement that has had a major effect on evangelical understandings of leadership.

32 Sarah Rowland Jones (ed.), *The Vision Before Us: The Kyoto Report of the Inter-Anglican Standing Commission on Ecumenical Relations*, 2000–2008, London: Anglican Communion Office, 2009.

33 George M. Marsden, *Reforming Fundamentalism: Fuller Seminary and the New Evangelicalism*, Grand Rapids, MI: Michigan, 1987, pp. 167ff.

The Church Growth Movement was pioneered by members of Fuller's School of World Mission. Its leading advocates there were Donald McGavran, Charles Kraft, Arthur Glasser and Peter Wagner. The defining feature of Church Growth Theory is the so-called Homogenous Unit Principle (HUP). As the Fuller group defined it, an HU can be classed as 'a section of society in which all members have some characteristic in common.'[34] This common characteristic could be identified as geographical, linguistic, ethnic, economic, social, or class-based, and the Fuller group began with the widely acknowledged assumption that societies regularly sub-divide into groups that are distinguished by such criteria. What made this 'Homogenous Unit' thinking into a 'Principle', however, was the group's assertion not only that congregations would grow more readily insofar as they observed such distinctions, but that the distinctions themselves were commensurate with the providence and purpose of God for the Church.[35]

As McGavran and his colleagues presented it, the primary justification for invoking the HUP is the fact that sociological barriers often inhibit people from conversion to Christ. Given that they have to cross a significant enough threshold in order to embrace the gospel as such, the Fuller group held that it would be unhelpful to suggest that they might then have to cross any *further* cultural thresholds to assimilate their new-found faith within the life of a congregation. As McGavran famously expressed it, people 'like to become Christians without crossing racial, linguistic or class barriers'.[36] Thus, whereas many existing churches might be *de facto* homogeneous units, those who adopted the HUP would seek *intentionally* to reach one particular section of society, on the assumption that a mission strategy focused in this way would achieve greater success than one that eschewed the targeting of specific demographic sectors.

---

34 John Stott (ed.), *The Pasadena Consultation: Homogeneous Unit*, Lausanne Occasional Papers No. 1, Wheaton, IL: Lausanne Committee for World Evangelization, 1977, p. 3.

35 Stott, *Pasadena Consultation*, p. 3.

36 Stott, *Pasadena Consultation*, p. 3.

By extension from all this, the Fuller group also suggested that church leaders who desired congregational growth would themselves strategise for it in accordance with the HUP – both by aligning to the common demographic characteristics of their congregations, and by commending HUP strategies in their preaching, teaching and decision-making. Thus, in the UK, as in many other Western contexts, a steady stream of books about leadership based on Church Growth principles has been produced over the past 30 years, from Eddie Gibbs' *I Believe in Church Growth* (1981) to Bob Jackson's *What Makes Churches Grow? Vision and Practice in Effective Evangelism* (2015).

Back in 1977, the Lausanne Committee on World Evangelization sponsored a special conference on the HUP at Pasadena, California, to consider its potential advantages and drawbacks. Supporters and opponents of the Principle each presented papers. In doing so, they did manage to find some common ground, not least in relation to the contingent nature of the principle as compared with God's ultimate purpose for the Church. Thus, one of the conclusions of the report produced from the conference read as follows:

> All of us are agreed that in many situations a homogeneous unit church can be a legitimate and authentic church. Yet we are also agreed that it can never be complete in itself. Indeed, if it remains in isolation, it cannot reflect the universality and diversity of the Body of Christ. Nor can it grow into maturity. Therefore, every HU church must take active steps to broaden its fellowship in order to demonstrate visibly the unity and variety of Christ's church. This will mean forging with each other and different churches creative relationships which express the reality of Christian love, brotherhood, and interdependence.[37]

On the positive side, the Pasadena report conceded to the Fuller group the point that the New Testament Church included relatively

---

37 Stott, *Pasadena Consultation*, p. 4.

monocultural congregations alongside more diverse ones: 'It seems probable', the text ran,

> that, although there were mixed Jewish–Gentile congregations, there were also homogeneous Jewish congregations (who still observed Jewish customs) and homogeneous Gentile congregations (who observed no Jewish customs).[38]

In the same vein, the participants were agreed that although Christ's death on the cross had abolished enmity between races and peoples (Eph. 2.15), 'this did not mean that Jews ceased to be Jews, or Gentiles to be Gentiles'.[39] Furthermore, even when viewed in its *eschatological* dimension, the Church as described in the New Testament would, the Pasadena report averred, remain a community in which 'the nations' and national identity would be distinguishable (Rev. 21.26; 22.2).[40] Yet despite these concessions, the critics of the HUP model were insistent that while cultural distinctions were not always bad in themselves, they were prone to sinful distortion and exploitation – not least in respect of racism. As such, they insisted that the HUP must always be subject to self-appraisal and, where necessary, to modification and qualification:

> To acknowledge the fact of HUs is not to acquiesce in the characteristics they possess which are displeasing to Christ. The Christian attitude to HUs is often called the 'realist attitude', because it realistically accepts that HUs exist and will always exist. We would prefer, however, to call this an attitude of 'dynamic realism' because we wish also to affirm that HUs can change and must always change. For Christ the Lord gives to his people new standards. They also receive a new homogeneity which transcends all others, for now they find their essential unity in Christ, rather than in culture.[41]

38 Stott, *Pasadena Consultation*, p. 4.

39 Stott, *Pasadena Consultation*, p. 4.

40 Stott, *Pasadena Consultation*, p. 7.

41 Stott, *Pasadena Consultation*, p. 6.

This tension between 'acquiescence' to temporal homogeneous units and obedience to the radically inclusive call of Christ goes to the very heart of debate about the Church's proper ecclesiology and missiology, as well to debates about the proper form and function of its leadership. It reflects the tension that lay at the centre of Paul's ministry – the tension between striving to be 'all things to all people' and resisting conformity to the world's 'mould' (1 Cor. 9.20–22; cf. Rom. 12.2).

Just as Peter Wagner helped to pioneer the model of the evangelical pastor or minister as Church Growth Strategist, so he also contributed to the development of the final key model of evangelical leadership in our survey – that of the 'Executive Archpastor'.

6. The Executive Archpastor

The 'Executive Archpastor' denotes a church leader who develops a national or international ministry from a single congregation, or from a local or regional network of congregations. Typically, as his or her church grows, the story of that growth is publicised and is offered as a pattern for others to emulate or adapt. Like the Parachurch Pioneer, the Executive Archpastor will characteristically itinerate to disseminate this story, but s/he will maintain oversight of his or her home church, albeit devolved in large measure to a team of others. This model of evangelical leadership is most conspicuously associated with North American 'megachurches': with Rick Warren's multi-million selling *Purpose-Driven Church* (1995), based on his ministry at Saddleback Church in Lake Forest, California; with Bill Hybels' *Courageous Leadership* (2002), rooted in his development of Willow Creek Community Church in South Barrington, Illinois, or – until his controversial resignation in 2014 – with Mark Driscoll's *On Church Leadership* (2008), which arose from his founding of Mars Hill Church in Seattle.[42]

---

42 Rick Warren, *The Purpose-Driven Church*, Grand Rapids, MI: Zondervan, 1995; Bill Hybels, *Courageous Leadership*, Grand Rapids MI: Zondervan, 2002; Mark Driscoll, *A Book You'll Actually Read on Church Leadership*, Wheaton, IL: Crossway, 2008. Driscoll's resignation over issues of 'church leadership and discipline' has been taken by some as indicative of the potential pitfalls of this model – see for example http://www.christianitytoday.com/ct/2014/october-web-only/mark-driscoll-resigns-from-mars-hill.html Accessed 30/10/15.

Executive Archpastors are typically in demand not only with church audiences but also in the business and civic worlds from which their leadership paradigms are in part derived. Here again, then, we see the activist/pragmatist dimension of Bebbington's quadrilateral at work.

In the Church of England context, the most successful transfer of this mainly American model so far occurred in the warm reception afforded to the ministry of John Wimber by several large Charismatic Evangelical Anglican churches and groupings in the 1980s and '90s – e.g. by St Michael-le-Belfrey, York, St Thomas', Crookes in Sheffield, St Andrew's, Chorleywood, and Holy Trinity, Brompton. Significantly, Wimber's demonstrative ministry of 'power evangelism', 'power healing', and 'signs and wonders' was developed with Peter Wagner at Fuller Seminary, and was closely bound up with the Church Growth principles that Wagner was defining with his faculty colleagues at the time.[43] Principally because of this, Steven Croft critiques its over-reliance on 'secular management theory' and specifically on Peter Drucker's 'management by objectives' paradigm, which, he argues, over-programmatises the church and over-managerialises the minister:

> The local church is (perhaps rightly) seen as systemic, that is, a complex organisation in which each part affects the other. However, the leap is then made to seeing the minister or senior pastor of a large church as the Chief Executive Officer ... As more people join the church, the minister becomes less and less of a pastor to individuals and more and more simply the supervisor and eventually the manager of a network of pastoral carers and other systems.[44]

---

43 For a detailed socio-theological analysis of Wimber's ministry see Martyn Percy, *Words, Wonders and Power: Understanding Contemporary Christian Fundamentalism and Revivalism*, London: SPCK, 1996.

44 Croft, *Ministry*, p. 24.

As Croft recounts it, the fact that these 'networks and systems' do not arise naturally from Scripture or church tradition but from commercial and industrial models means that over time he became uneasy with them. Yet as we have seen, the interplay between 'secular' and 'sacred' models of leadership has been a feature of Evangelicalism from its earliest days, and in any case it might be argued – on evangelical grounds – that too stark a contrast between these different sources risks denying the sovereignty of God over the whole of creation in general, and over human systems of leadership in particular. No doubt Evangelicalism's tendency to reduce the fine distinctions between biblical ministries into generic patterns of 'leadership' might at times overlook vital subtleties in the providence of God. Yet as biblical commentators routinely point out, not all of those distinctions are clear,[45] and the hermeneutical task of interpreting and applying them to the church in the world of today may not be so straightforward.

45 See e.g. Eduard Schweizer, *Church Order in the New Testament,* London: SCM, 1961; C.K. Barrett, *Church, Ministry and Sacraments in the New Testament,* Eugene, OR: Wipf & Stock, 1985, pp.54–76; David W. Bennett, *Metaphors of Ministry: Biblical Images for Leaders and Followers*, Grand Rapids, MI: Baker / Carlisle: Paternoster, 1993; James D.G. Dunn, *Unity and Diversity in the New Testament: An Inquiry into the Character of Earliest Christianity* (3rd edn), London: SCM, 2006; Derek Tidball, *Ministry by the Book: New Testament Patterns for Pastoral Leadership,* Nottingham: Apollos, 2008.

Part 3

Continuing the Conversation

3.1 Faithful Improvisation or Talent Management? A Conversation between the FAOC report and the Green Report[1]

Mike Higton

The Faith and Order Commission's report on Senior Church Leadership appeared in public shortly after another report on a similar topic: the Report of the Lord Green Steering Group, or 'Talent Management for Future Leaders and Leadership Development for Bishops and Deans: A New Approach'[2] – a report widely criticised in church newspaper comment pieces and letters pages, and on multiple blogs.[3] Thanks to the coincidence in timing, the FAOC report was understood by some as itself a critique of or alternative to the 'Green Report' (as it became known), even though its origins were independent of, and much earlier than, those of the Green Report, and the processes by which the two were written had

1 This chapter is a shortened and updated version of a series of five blog posts written in February 2015. The last, which links to all the others, is available at mikehigton.org.uk/re-reading-the-green-report-5-management/

2 Available online at churchofengland.org/media/2130591/report.pdf; it has also been published as a Synod paper, with an introductory summary, at www.churchofengland.org/media/2141121/gs%201982%20-%20discerning%20and%20nurturing%20senior%20leaders.pdf. The initial Church Times report is available at www.churchtimes.co.uk/articles/2014/12- december/news/uk/plan-to-groom-talent-for-high-office-in-c-of-e

3 Various collections of responses to the Green Report have been gathered by the Thinking Anglicans blog: www.thinkinganglicans.org.uk/archives/006806.html; www.thinkinganglicans.org.uk/archives/006816.html; www.thinkinganglicans.org.uk/archives/006827.html; and www.thinkinganglicans.org.uk/archives/006833.html.)

been largely independent. The confusion was, nevertheless, understandable. After all, the FAOC report asks whether 'the appropriation of leadership language from secular sources been sufficiently critical?' (§37), and the main criticism directed at the Green Report by its critics was precisely that its appropriation of this language had *not* been sufficiently critical. When, in §8, the report's authors claimed that its recommendations marked 'a culture change for the leadership of the Church', critics therefore feared that the change in question was a takeover of the church by the corporate world. Martyn Percy, in a critique published in the *Church Times*, suggested that the Report offered 'a dish of basic contemporary approaches to executive management, with a little theological garnish'.[4]

It is worth, however, bringing the two reports into conversation, precisely on this topic of the relationship between theological and corporate language. The language of the Green Report certainly leant towards the corporate from very early on, with talk of 'talent management initiatives', and so on, but it did contain substantial strands of theological language woven in with its corporate language. In what follows, with the help of the FAOC report, I ask what picture emerges if we take those theological strands to be central. I'm not ignoring the critical readings; I agree that there are times when the report's language pulls quite sharply against this theological reading, and when this theological reading therefore calls for some revision. The attempt is nevertheless a task that the report itself encouraged. Very close to the end, in §85, the report noted that it had used 'corporate labels such as "talent management", "leadership development programme", "talent pool" and "alumni network"', and acknowledges that 'these should perhaps be replaced by terms meaningful to the Church' – a suggestion that was put into practice as soon as the Report's recommendations began to be implemented.

4 See www.churchtimes.co.uk/articles/2014/12-december/comment/opinion/are-these-the-leaders-that-we-really-want

My attempt to read the report theologically is, in part, an attempt to think through the rationale for that process, and to identify what is at stake in it.

Faithful Improvisation and Prayer

We can begin with the most obvious link between the two reports. The main body of the Green Report started (in §10) with a quotation from Justin Welby's first address to the General Synod as Archbishop of Canterbury, in July 2013. He spoke of the members of the Church being 'Custodians of the gospel that transforms individuals and societies ... called by God to respond radically and imaginatively to new contexts.' That word 'custodian' suggests that we hold faithfully to what we have received; the reference to imaginative and radical response suggests that this faithfulness will be expressed in new ways in new contexts. The connection to the FAOC report is made explicit just a couple of paragraphs later: 'The Faith and Order Commission's document on leadership speaks of "faithful improvisation" as a key characteristic of Christian leadership. This is exactly what this plan promotes' (§14).

In the FAOC report, we said (§§12–13) that compelling answers to questions about the kind of senior leadership needed by the Church of England

> are not developed in the pages of reports. They are developed *in situ*, hammered out in context by Christians drawing deeply on the Scriptures, engaging with the tradition, attending to their situations, questioning and challenging and encouraging one another, and discovering prayerfully over time what bears fruit and what does not. In other words, good answers to this question are produced by faithful improvisation, in the never-ending diversity of contexts in which the church finds itself ... Musicians who are deeply trained in a particular tradition (who know its constraints and possibilities in their bones) draw on all the resources provided by that formation to respond

> creatively to new situations and to one another. Compelling and faithful answers to the church's questions about leadership require something of the same deep formation and deep attentiveness *in situ*, and will be similarly diverse and creative.

We therefore (§174) spoke of 'constant, prayerful, humble and attentive listening by the whole church, and especially by those who exercise leadership within it, to what the Spirit may be saying to God's people' because 'Wise improvisation in leadership will ... only emerge from communities and individuals gathered by the Spirit in sustained prayer and worship, with the Son, before the Father.'

The Green Report similarly insisted that faithfully improvisatory leadership must be rooted in prayer. It talked about the importance of the leaders' 'life of prayer' (§10); a substantial element of prayer was built into the proposed patterns of training (§35); and the diagram of 'Leadership Characteristics for Bishops and Deans' (§32) had at its top this statement of 'purpose': 'Develop a prayerful cadre of Bishops and Deans who are confident as leaders and evangelists who release an energy for mission and growth across the Church, as the urgent priority set by the Gospel' (see also §10).

All our action, including any action we call 'leadership', is a joining in, a participation in what God is doing. As the FAOC report says elsewhere, 'one's action is a gift that one receives more than it is something that one achieves; [and] there can be no effectiveness without grace' (§48). Prayer is the starting point not simply because we need to seek guidance before acting, or to recharge batteries before expending energy. It is the starting point because our agency – our determination, our endeavour, our action – is never primary. Our vision of ministry, and of leadership within it, should not begin with any picture of heroic activity on the part of those who minister, but of deep and abiding receptivity and attentiveness. To minister is to be acted upon by God, to be caught up in what God is doing in and through us. Its centre is not labour (though there is certain to be labour involved), but rest in God. Prayer is therefore necessarily the centre of ministry, including of all those forms of ministry that we call leadership.

The training programme instigated following the Green Report has prayer and reflection as one of its major components. To fulfil its promise, that has to be more than simply a space for prayerful reflection on what has been learnt, however. Rather, central to the substance of the training, there has to be a focus upon developing and sustaining the kinds of habit of prayer, the kinds of community of prayer, the kinds of rule of prayerful life, that can underpin the kinds of ministry envisaged.

Confidence

The FAOC report insists that

> The growth of God's kingdom is in God's hands. We must pray all we can, learn all we can and work all we can, but these are not handles that need only to be turned hard to guarantee success. (§185)

Our future is in God's hands. That does not mean that we don't need to act strenuously in the present, but it does mean that we need to act not out of anxiety and panic, but out of trust: wholehearted reliance upon God.

When the Green report spoke of 'confidence' (as in 'a prayerful cadre of Bishops and Deans who are confident as leaders and evangelists'), we should therefore read this first of all not as self-confidence, but as confidence in God. As §15 says, 'This confidence is rooted entirely in the victory of Christ.' It is the confidence that flows from prayer, and so from trust in God, from rest in God. But God's action and our action are not in competition, and to focus on God's action does not mean that we have to deny our own. God's action enables, accompanies and directs our own, and a primary confidence in God is compatible with a secondary confidence in ourselves – what the Green report calls a 'realistic confidence' in our ability (§13) – a thankfulness for the gifts that God has given us, a practised knowledge in their possibilities and limits, and a joy in their exercise.

Our confidence in ourselves is, however, bounded by our confidence in God. Our self-confidence must never become a conviction that we are the centre of what is going on. It has to be a self-confidence that remains attentive to what God is doing beyond us and without us, ready for surprises, and open to correction. It has to be a self-confidence that does not let us take ourselves too seriously. As the Green Report said, 'We want leaders so centred on God that they exhibit neither neurosis nor narcissism' (§17), and finding that balance in the context of a demanding ministry is a serious spiritual discipline.

One aspect of the 'culture change' that the Green report spoke of (§8) should therefore to be a move away from a culture of anxiety. On the one hand, that means a move away from a culture of communal anxiety about the future of the Church – as if everything depended upon us. On the other hand, it means a move away from a culture of individual performance anxiety – as if the one thing needful is to make a success of ourselves, to demonstrate our worth by what we achieve. Confidence in God is the root of a move away from such ecclesial Pelagianism – and it is the root of the joy, resilience, energy, and hope of which the Green Report spoke (§12).

The Green Report therefore rightly warned against the aversion to risk that can flow from the belief that we can manage risk away (§22). Instead, the church needs 'spaces of safe uncertainty in which creative and emotionally intelligent change can happen.' A move away from a culture dominated by anxiety and control is necessary if faithful improvisation is going to flourish. Micromanagement kills improvisation; insecurity kills improvisation; fear of failure, the need to perform, the obsession with targets, all kill improvisation.

Promoting 'safe uncertainty' means refusing a culture focused on success. As we said in the FAOC report:

> We therefore have to cultivate a culture that allows failure, that attends to it carefully and learns from it seriously, but that does not condemn it. In part, this is because we will certainly not encourage real improvisation and experimentation if we have generated an atmosphere of performance anxiety; improvisation is only made possible by trust. More seriously, however, it is because any understanding of Christian leadership that believes success to be firmly in the grasp of good leaders, rather than in the hands of God, has become a form of idolatry. The one true leader of the church is God, Father, Son and Holy Spirit, and true success is in God's hands alone. (§186)

Leadership in the Body

The words 'lead', 'leader' and 'leadership' and their derivatives were used on every page of the Green Report. In the FAOC report, we looked at the rise and rise of leadership language in the Church (§§18–23), and concluded that

> this language is not going away any time soon. It has simply become too prevalent and too deeply embedded, and we acknowledge that this is in part because it can name important needs in the church's life. Rather than arguing about whether we should stop using leadership language, therefore, we discuss how this language might be used well (§10)

because

> It can only be right to make 'leadership' a central idea in the life of the church if our ideas and practices of leadership ... are subjected to ongoing critical questioning in the light of the church's relation to its Lord. (§168)

We claimed that it is

> impossible to sustain a simple opposition between Christian and secular ideas of leadership. Our tradition has always been

> in the business of assimilating and transforming material from the world around it ... The only interesting questions are about the kind and depth of the transformation and assimilation involved, not about the fact of borrowing itself. (§164)

What, though, do we mean by 'leadership'? We offered an 'initial, low-key definition':

> We might say that a leader is someone who assists others in the performance of a collective practice. Such a leader is not necessarily one who himself or herself excels in the practice, though he or she certainly has to be competent in it. Rather, he or she will be good at participating in that practice in such a way as to draw others deeper into it. (§39)

If that is where we start, however, we immediately have to reject any simplistic division of the Body of Christ into 'leaders' and 'led'. Paul says in 1 Corinthians 12.7 that 'To each is given the manifestation of the Spirit for the common good.' We need each other; we are built up by each other; we assist each other in the growth and enactment of our faith. Starting with the low-key definition of 'leadership' above, we would have to conclude (as a first move) that leadership is something in which we are all involved or called to be involved.

We shouldn't, therefore, envisage a division between leaders and led, but a complex ecology of multiple forms of assistance and encouragement, building up the whole body together. (As we said in the FAOC report, §177, 'Even the ministry of oversight, of *episkope*, is first of all a ministry of all God's people, who are called to exercise self-control and hold one another to account.') We can certainly recognise many forms of *differentiation* – different gifts, callings, talents distributed around the body – but they are all differentiations within a Body in which every member is called to minister, to encourage, to assist.

It is therefore appropriate that the statement of purpose at the top of the Green Report's diagram of Leadership Characteristics (§32) described leaders who 'release an energy for mission and growth across the Church, as the urgent priority set by the Gospel'. In the light of the FAOC report, we will read this not as the high-octane energy of the big leader, but as the energy that flows in each of us from a confident, trusting participation in what God is doing, grounded in prayer. This is not an energy that a few possess and then distribute to others. Neither, however, is it simply an energy independently found in each of us. Our relationships of trust and confidence in God are never simply about the individual and God. We encourage one another, we build one another up, and we are involved in one another's relation to God. That is what it means to be a body. The Spirit's work in each of us is inseparable from the Spirit's work in those around us, and we can therefore all be involved in the 'release' of energy of the Spirit in those around us.

Minding our Language

The Green report did not simply talk about mutual encouragement, however. It talked about a *cadre of leaders* who will be engaged in this work of encouragement. It focused on Bishops and Deans, but also talked about 'heads of theological colleges, mission agencies, para-church networks or significant pilgrimage centres' and leaders of 'large churches with specially significant roles in national church life' (§64). Even here, though, if we start with the vision of the Body of Christ sketched above, we won't think of these people as 'the leaders' over against everyone else as 'the led'. We won't think of them as people who have come out on top of some hierarchy of excellence or importance or value. Rather, we will simply recognise that, in the midst of a Body in which every member is called to minister, some people have received a specific kind of calling which involves ministry to a large geographical area, or playing a significant role in relation to a large number of people, as well as (in some of those cases) playing specific sacramental roles and specific representative roles – and so having a role in the encouragement and enabling of the ministry of a large number of other members of the Body. To be called into these roles is not promotion; it is not a form of elevation. Even 'seniority' is potentially a very misleading word for it. It is, rather, a call to occupy one specific niche in the overall ecology of the Church's ministry.

Training specifically aimed at enabling the holders of these posts to develop in what they do therefore has to strike a careful balance. On the one hand, it might well make sense, for some developmental purposes, to take them out of their contexts and bring them together as a cohort, in order for them to share the wisdom and experience they have gained in similar roles, and in order for them to receive appropriate training in how to face common challenges. In the same way, we might bring together people involved in similar ministries in all sorts of other niches of the church's ecology; there's nothing specifically 'senior' about this idea. On the other hand, we should guard against any sense that those being brought together are a breed apart, or even an elite, separating off into their own exclusive club. They are brought together as a cohort *for the sake of* their distinctive involvement in the overall weave of ministry that they share with others, and in order to energise and refresh them for deeper engagement with those around them, wider collaboration, and a fuller sharing of the tasks of ministry. Any programme of leadership development needs to be carefully handled, if it is not to encourage any sense of isolation or exclusivity.

In the light of all this, there are elements of the Green Report's language that do, I think, require the kind of critical approach that the FAOC report recommends before the Church adopts the language of the corporate world – and, indeed, that critical approach has been evident in the way that the language has evolved as the Report has been implemented. The term 'talent pool', for instance, was quickly dropped, and was replaced with 'learning community'.

First, from time to time, the language it used to discuss leadership could indeed have suggested that leaders were a race apart. Take that word 'cadre', for instance, in the statement of purpose (§32). The dictionary definition, 'a small group of people specially trained for a particular purpose', is not itself problematic, but it sounded to my ears all too like a group defined over against their surroundings (the group of army officers who have their own mess; the closed communist cell that is working against the surrounding bourgeois society).

Second, and more pervasively, the Report used language that moved away from a simple *differentiation* of ministries and towards a *hierarchy of value*. We were, it seems, to look for 'exceptional individuals' (§6), 'candidates with exceptional potential' (§10), 'exceptional potential leaders from among the clergy' (§12); people who demonstrate 'exceptional performance' (§49) – and so on. It was hard not to read this as suggesting that we were indeed talking about promotion, about climbing a hierarchy with the best and brightest at the top.

This is where, to echo the FAOC report, we need to 'question what ways of thinking the church might inadvertently have borrowed when it took on this vocabulary' (§37). We are certainly looking out for people who are exceptionally well suited for the specific ministries that we have in mind – but only in the sense that we might also look for people who are exceptionally well suited to be a welcomer at the church door, or who are exceptionally well suited to staff the night shift at the homeless shelter. That is, we are trying to discern together to what roles, to what forms of ministry, God is calling each person; we are trying to discern where every person best fits in the activity of the body, in ways that will do most justice to the specific gifts – the specific talents – that God has given to each of them.

That is why the Green Report rightly said that a Bishop or a Dean will be someone who 'Recognises and develops unique gifts' and who is 'a creative steward of lay and ordained talent' (§32); someone who will give priority to 'Supporting the formation and development of individuals in the full range of their ministry' (§10). The Bishop or Dean is one minister in a whole church of ministers, a person with one peculiar set of talents amongst the talents of all those who make up the church, who pursues his or her ministry only in relation to the ministry of others.

Discernment

The Green Report, then, is focused on certain specific niches in the overall ecology of the Church's ministry – Bishops and Deans in the first instance, but also various other roles with a particular kind of public visibility, or roles which require working on an unusually large scale. Those niches do exist in the life of the church, and they do from time to time need filling. We do therefore need some processes by which we discern together who will best fill those niches, and provide them with the support and development needed to fill them well.

These are not things that, on the whole, the church has done well in its recent history, and the Green Report therefore sketches a process that will be 'more open to the emergence of leaders from a wider variety of backgrounds and range of skills than is currently predictable' (§11), and more transparent and accountable.

A great deal of the process set out in the Green Report rested upon the Development and Appointments Group (DAG), who were given the task of determining who participates in the process (§49). Their remit is, therefore, to oversee the church's discernment process for a specific range of peculiar roles – just one discernment process amongst the many that the church needs. Discernment is, however, fundamentally an activity of the whole church (see the FAOC report, §182). We open each other's eyes to see better; we test each other's discernments, and the truthfulness of our discernment emerges, God willing, from this interaction. As DAG's role continues to develop, therefore, it and all those who relate to it will need to go on looking for ways in which its work can be informed as richly as possible, and challenged as deeply as possible, by the discernment of others – the challenging wisdom of the Body. DAG is there to gather and to reflect on (and be surprised and challenged by) the discernment of others – both about who they should be looking for and about what they should be looking for. It is there to search diligently, prayerfully and humbly for the signs of what God is doing, by listening long and hard to those around it in the church.

At times, as the Green Report itself suggests, that will mean being open to real surprise: 'The Church must be more intentional about drawing in those with high potential who do not appear to "fit in"' (§11). We are, after all, seeking to discern together the movement of the Spirit of God, not seeking ways to secure the continuation of our own plans. Discernment is therefore properly a two-directional process. On the one hand, there is the process of the church discerning who might be the right person to fit into the space we want to fill. On the other, there is the process of discerning how our sense of the shape of that space might be changed by the people whom God is sending us. It is a process in which the church is seeking to be discerning about itself and its future, as well as about the future ministries of specific individuals.

The Green Report's language of monitoring, of evaluation, and of benchmarking could, if given the wrong kind of priority, work against this. The task of discernment entrusted to DAG is one that demands as much creativity as measurement. As its role continues to develop, it and all those who relate to it will need to go on looking for ways in which the church can both take seriously the known demands imposed by these specific roles, and the unexpected and sometimes disruptive ways in which God can fit people for them.

The Green Report already contains the key insight that calls into question too controlling a vision of measurement. In §14, it says that 'God's wisdom is our measure of how we learn to manage better'; in §24 it speaks of 'the measure of the full stature of Christ'. As the FAOC report says,

> It is always worth asking whether our descriptions of leadership can leave room for a leader who was abandoned by all his followers, who was stripped of all dignity and power, and whose ministry was in every measurable sense defeated –

> and where that failure was nevertheless the foundation stone of God's mission. (§49)

The work of discernment is always, at its deepest, the work of discovering how the God of Jesus Christ is working amongst us, and that's never going to be a process that we can make predictable and safe. It is (or should be) a spiritual discipline, rooted in prayer. That does not simply mean the prayerfulness of the individuals involved, nor simply in the opening and closing of our meetings with prayer, but in the recognition that the whole business of discernment – of discovering how the God of Jesus Christ is working amongst us – is a form of prayer, a spiritual discipline. We have, I suspect, a good deal to learn – from everyone from Jesuits to Quakers, as well as from our own tradition – about how such a form of prayer can flourish.

As Justin Welby has said, 'If we want to see things changed, it starts with prayer. It starts with a new spirit of prayer, using all the traditions, ancient and modern' – because there can be 'No renewal of the Church without renewal of prayer.'[5]

5 See www.archbishopofcanterbury.org/pages/roles-and-priorities.html#Prayer%201, and www.archbishopofcanterbury.org/articles.php/5359/no-renewal-of-the-church-without-renewal-of-prayer-archbishop-in-south-africa.

3.2 Creating Meaning Together

Tim Harle

I am grateful for this opportunity to reflect on the FAOC *Senior Church Leadership* report from my experience in the professional world of leadership development, both inside and outside the church. A quote from the work that gives the chapter its title frames this response. Preben Friis is a Danish actor who bridges two traditions (acting and management) in a way that evokes the traditions of theology and leadership we are considering. Improvisation certainly provides a link.

> When we improvise, we are spontaneously responding to each other's gestures, and thus we do not know the full meaning of what we are doing until we have done it. The meaning emerges through the process of having intentions, acting and getting responses. This is a social process, where we are creating meaning together in what we are doing in the act of doing it ... The paradox of improvising means acting in two apparently opposite ways: being skilled and experienced in what you are doing, and at the same time acting spontaneously. This is knowing and not-knowing simultaneously.[1]

My response to the FAOC report distilled initially into three main areas: I first consider these, then examine a number of connections prompted by the report, before concluding with an invitation.

---

1 Preben Friis, 'Presence and Spontaneity in Improvisational Work', in Patricia Shaw and Ralph Stacey (eds), *Experiencing Risk, Spontaneity and Improvisation in Organizational Change: Working Live*, Abingdon: Routledge, 2006, pp. 75–94. The quote is from p. 86.

Initial Responses

Senior Leadership?

My immediate response relates to the report's title. I am familiar with the contested concept of leadership, I meet people described as senior leaders, but senior leadership is a term I struggled with. My work in leadership development continually searches out the potential in people who may not consider themselves leaders. Leadership is something we should find at the top, in the middle, and at the edges of organisations.[2]

This leads to a second point. Leadership development programmes work best when there is close engagement between senior leaders and others at different levels. This may take the form of a cohort made up of a 'diagonal slice' across an organisation. I saw an excellent example of this in a European financial services organisation, where an Executive Vice-President would take part in all learning activities (including group activities) alongside a mix of executives and middle managers. Contrast this with a British public sector organisation, where the Chief Executive sent an email apologising for their absence along the lines of, 'This programme is vital to our future, and I encourage you to engage with it. But I'm too busy to take part myself.'

Leaders need to be ready to show deep engagement, and vulnerability, as part of their – and their organisation's – learning process. One practical rider to this is to recognise that the presence of senior leader(s) from within the same organisation may stifle open conversation.

---

2 Joseph A. Raelin, *Creating Leaderful Organizations: How to Bring Out Leadership in Everyone*, San Francisco, CA: Berrett-Koehler, 2003.

We Need Theologians

My second response to the FAOC report was to welcome the theological reflection that lies behind it, but to be frustrated that the commission did not engage with thinking about leadership beyond churches. The report rightly notes the importance of neither dismissing 'secular' leadership approaches nor uncritically baptising anything that appears in the *Harvard Business Review.*

My experience at a number of (avowedly secular) business schools in Europe, North America and Australasia is that contributions from spiritual and faith traditions can be welcomed. Recognising the failure of much that has gone before, Gary Hamel from London Business School makes this plea:

> we need more than engineers and accountants. We must also harness the ideas of artists, philosophers, designers, ecologists, anthropologists, and theologians.[3]

This reflection indicates some areas where cross-boundary conversations may lead to deeper learning about leadership.

Faithful Improvisation

One phrase, for me, leapt out from the pages of *Senior Church Leadership*. Faithful improvisation evoked a series of avenues to explore. As I understand the report, faithful improvisation relates both to organisational forms and leadership roles that the church may take in differing times and places, and also to one of the crucial attitudes that should be seen in leaders. This is remarkably close to key ideas coming from the business leadership community.

One of the earliest proponents of an improvisational approach was Henry Mintzberg, writing about strategic planning. But I want to

---

3 Gary Hamel, *What Matters Now: How to Win in a World of Relentless Change, Ferocious Competition, and Unstoppable Innovation*, San Francisco, CA: Jossey-Bass, 2012, p. 254.

concentrate on two authors. Frank Barrett is a Professor of Management and a jazz musician. In *Yes to the Mess*, Barrett writes how he 'realised that jazz is more than a metaphor for organising. Jazz bands actually *are* organisations designed for innovation.'[4] He emphasises the importance of mindsets and culture, and draws particular attention to the significance of complexity theory through such authors as Ralph Stacey and Meg Wheatley. Building on VISA founder Dee Hock's concept of chaordic systems, Barrett notes that *'systems are most creative when they operate with a combination of order and chaos.'*[5]

The idea of jazz as a model is not new among senior Anglican leaders,[6] though note how Barrett pleads for us to move beyond metaphor. This raises important questions about our attitudes to order, authority and control. But first we need to discuss the second concept highlighted by faithful improvisation.

Bricolage as a term in organisational studies was first introduced by the anthropologist Claude Lévi-Strauss. Its use in leadership circles has been promoted by Keith Grint, Professor of Public Leadership at Warwick Business School.[7] As with jazz, so with bricolage: Anglicans have heard this before. Martyn Percy builds on Elaine Graham's work to apply bricolage to leadership in the Church of England.[8] Questions of culture, identity and learning are interwoven in this approach.

---

4 Frank J. Barrett, *Yes to the Mess: Surprising Leadership Lessons from Jazz*, Boston, MA: Harvard Business Review Press, 2012, p. x, italics in the original.

5 Barrett, *Yes to the Mess*, p. 70, italics original.

6 John Gladwin, 'Team Leadership as Jazz', in *Exploring Team Leadership*, York: Foundation for Church Leadership, 2007, p. 34.

7 Keith Grint, 'Wicked Problems and Clumsy Solutions: the Role of Leadership', *Clinical Leader* 1.2 (2008), pp. 54–68.

8 Martyn Percy, *Anglicanism: Confidence, Commitment and Communion*, Farnham: Ashgate, 2013, pp. 143ff.

Connections

I now look at the FAOC report to highlight areas where connections can be made with leadership development beyond the church. Extracts are necessarily selective, and certainly cannot claim to be exhaustive. But I hope they indicate fruitful ground for future conversations.

For and Against Leadership (Section 2)

§16 explores the connection between **leadership and church growth**. A widely read business book is Jim Collins' *Good to Great.* Collins identifies a link between Chief Executives, who demonstrate 'a paradoxical blend of personal humility and professional will,' and enduring success for the corporations they lead. One of the criticisms of Collins is that these Chief Executives found themselves at the top of enduring companies at a time when success came (perhaps due to shifts in the market). Collins demonstrated a link, but critics challenge whether it is a causal one.[9]

Senior Church Leadership draws attention to the rise of **leadership language** in the 1980s (Section 2.1). Pivotal to this development was a 1977 *Harvard Business Review* article, which posed the question, Management and Leadership: Are They Different? Abraham Zaleznik answered with an emphatic, Yes. This opened the floodgates for consultants encouraging us to aspire to be leaders. Management was for the 'also rans'. John Adair subsequently described this as the Zaleznik Error: 'the making of a false dichotomy between "leaders" and "managers"'.[10] One of my favourite articles

9 Jim Collins, *Good to Great: Why Some Companies Make the Leap ... and Others Don't*, London: Random House, 2001. The quote is from p. 20. I have found Collins' identification of the 'paradoxical blend' helpful in countering expectations from aspiring leaders that they have to be larger-than-life charismatics. See also Dennis Tourish, *The Dark Side of Transformational Leadership: A Critical Perspective*, Hove: Routledge, 2013.

10 John Adair, *How to Grow Leaders: The Seven Key Principles of Effective Leadership Development*, London: Kogan Page, 2005, p. 64.

suggests that leadership involves 'the extra-ordinarisation of the mundane', a concept with incarnational resonance.[11]

The Modem network, which describes itself as "hub for leadership, management and ministry" (www.modem-uk.org), could be mentioned as an example of **two-way learning** (§36 footnote 11). I convened a group of consultants, clergy and business school academics to identify the best contemporary leadership books. The conversations that took place before and after publication of our list were every bit as important as the list itself.[12] This is an example of the type of conversation I am advocating here.

Learning from Monastic Traditions

Reference to the Rule of St Benedict (§§138f) prompts two connections with leadership development in business circles. First, there has been a growing interest in monastic rules, especially that of Benedict.[13] A more recent book blends a contemporary US business entrepreneurial approach with the Trappist tradition.[14] One reason may be the way these traditions hold interesting opposites in tension: individual and community, organisation and freedom, sacred and secular.

A particular favourite of mine from Benedict's Rule is highlighted in the FAOC report (§139). The opportunity for the youngest to show the way points to two aspects of leadership development:

---

11 Mats Alvesson and Stefan Sveningsson, 'Managers Doing Leadership: The Extra-ordinarization of the Mundane', *Human Relations* 56.12 (2003), pp. 1435–59.

12 The best leadership books report can be downloaded from www.modem-uk.org/bestbooks.html.

13 Kit Dollard, Anthony Marett-Crosby and Timothy Wright, *Doing Business with Benedict: The Rule of Saint Benedict and Business Management: a Conversation*, London: Continuum, 2002.

14 August Turak, *Business Secrets of the Trappist Monks: One CEO's Quest for Meaning and Authenticity*, New York, NY: Columbia Business School Publishing, 2013. A favourite personal memory comes from a symposium I attended at the Vlerick Business School in Belgium. A contributor from the Trappist tradition spoke for three minutes, then paused for three minutes of silence, before resuming. This pattern stimulated some participants, but unnerved others.

15 Keith Grint, *Leadership: Limits and Possibilities*, Basingstoke: Palgrave, 2005, pp. 103ff.

Inverse learning. Keith Grint first drew attention to this phenomenon, observed on a RAF training course.[15] Noting how parents learn from their children, Grint goes on to suggest how followers may become teachers to leaders. This highlights leadership development as a community, rather than individual, activity.

Reverse mentoring. The idea that more senior (in age or authority) leaders need to learn from younger colleagues is becoming more widespread in business.[16] A keen proponent is the IDEO design consultancy. In churches, Earl Creps argues 'that reverse mentoring is one of the disciplines crucial to being wise.'[17] I can vouch for the benefits of reverse mentoring, through insights I receive from a twenty-something student.

The organisation (§§33, 149)

An under-represented aspect of leadership in church circles is that which addresses the organisational level. The great majority of programmes and books concentrate on the individual leader. Teamwork will probably be mentioned, but the organisational perspective rarely is. A welcome exception to this rule is Keith Elford, who applies the Viable Systems Model to churches.[18]

The **local and trans-local** are mentioned in various places (§§ 63, 177). Churches are not alone in dealing with such challenges, as any transnational corporation or international charity can attest. I have found the concept of fractals helpful here: repeating, scale-free patterns observed at many levels. Activities of leaders may vary,

---

16 Ronald Alsop, 'Young mentors teach "old dogs" new tricks' (2014), http://www.bbc.com/capital/story/20140311-meet-your-mentor-hes-just-24. Accessed 31/10/15.

17 Earl Creps, *Reverse Mentoring: How Young Leaders Can Transform the Church and Why We Should Let Them*, San Francisco, CA: Jossey-Bass, 2008, p. 62.

18 Keith Elford, *Creating the Future of the Church: A Practical Guide to Addressing Whole-System Change*, London: SPCK, 2013.

but there should be a recognisable pattern in how they approach their work.[19]

Approaching Change

The reference to the need for 'continual transformation' (§ 141) points in two directions. First, to the Benedictine vow of conversion of life. Secondly, to a challenge from Gary Hamel and CK Prahalad:

> Enormous managerial energy ... [has] been devoted to turnarounds, rescues, and massive 'change' programs, yet isn't the real goal to avoid a crisis-sized transformation problem by creating a capacity for continuous renewal deep within the company?[20]

If churches cannot address questions of continuous renewal deep within, who can?

At various stages in its report, FAOC draws attention to a creative tension between **order and chaos** (e.g. Improvising within a Tradition (Section 5.8)). I am struck by the work of Professor Mary Uhl-Bien. Despite winning an award from *Leadership Quarterly* for an earlier paper applying complexity theory to leadership, she prefers a subsequent paper,[21] which acknowledges the need for a judicious mix of a complexity approach and something reminiscent of Weber's classic work on bureaucracy.

---

19 Tim Harle, 'Fractal Leadership: Emerging Patterns for Transformation', in Joann Danelo Barbour and Gill Robinson Hickman (eds), *Leadership for Transformation*, San Francisco, CA: Jossey-Bass, 2011, pp. 33–49.

20 Gary Hamel and C.K. Prahalad, *Competing for the Future*, revised edn, Boston, MA: Harvard Business Press, 1996, p. x.

21 Mary Uhl-Bien and Russ Marion 'Complexity Leadership in Bureaucratic Forms of Organizing: A Meso Model', *Leadership Quarterly* 20.4 (2009), pp. 631–50.

Individual Leaders and their Communities

Vocation (§§ 57, 157). I am reminded of Rakesh Khurana's devastating critique of the North American Business School tradition. Contrasting early noble aims of following in the footsteps of Harvard Schools of Law, and indeed Divinity, Khurana notes the sad decline from 'higher aims' to churning out 'hired hands'.[22] Surely churches can urge potential leaders in businesses and other settings to rediscover the concept of a calling or vocation.

The quotation from the *Working as One Body* report that, 'God has given outstanding skills of leadership to particular individuals' (§21) raises a number of questions. Should the focus be on individuals? And, in particular, is the reference to **skills** correct? Leadership development programmes are littered with competency frameworks, yet how often do these miss out crucial aspects of leadership. The epithet, 'we recruit for character and train for skills' is a clumsy way of making the same point.

The topics of **vulnerability** (§§ 48, 185) and **failure** (§§185, 186) are areas where the church can contribute to conversations about leadership through the less-than-perfect. We need the leadership equivalent of Henri Nouwen's *Wounded Healer*. Mention of failure cannot pass without drawing attention to lessons from nature, where failure is crucial to development both in the evolutionary record and in contemporary cycles of growth and decay.[23] Participants on leadership development courses tell me that such approaches are welcome. In this context, how refreshing it is to see the language of fruit being used (§169), rather than outputs or outcomes.

---

22 Rakesh Khurana, *From Higher Aims to Hired Hands: The Social Transformation of American Business Schools and the Unfulfilled Promise of Management as a Profession*, Princeton, NJ: Princeton University Press, 2007.

23 Tim Harle, 'Contemplating Compost: Leadership Lessons from Nature', *The Bible in TransMission*, Summer 2015, pp. 17–19.

Theology

With some trepidation, I venture to suggest that the FAOC report could have explored fundamental theology even further than it did. I offer two examples.

First, the Trinity. This is referenced through a Pauline lens (§56). My experience suggests that we have much to learn from a social model. Robin Greenwood expresses this well: 'In a trinitarian ecclesiology, order is not provided or imposed by a single group, permanently over against another, but by the fluctuating movement in relationship of the personal participants ... In a perichoretic community of love, a self-ordering process takes place in which, although individual persons will fulfil unique and necessary roles, the total ordering is achieved without any one being in a permanently subordinate position to another.'[24]

Secondly, does *Senior Church Leadership* reflect an implicit rational Western scientific worldview of cause and effect in its understanding of leadership, which in turn reflects the nature of the deity? If there is one approach that participants on leadership development programmes appreciate, it is one that learns from recent developments around complexity science. Emergence and self-organisation realise more potential than attempts to control chaos. An emergent reading of the first creation story in Genesis provides a good starting point.[25]

---

24 Robin Greenwood, *Transforming Priesthood: A New Theology of Mission and Ministry*, London: SPCK, 1994, p. 152. See also Stephen Pickard, *Theological Foundations for Collaborative Ministry*, Farnham: Ashgate, 2009.

25 Catherine Keller, *Face of the Deep: A Theology of Becoming*, Abingdon: Routledge, 2003.

An Invitation from the World of Leadership to the Churches

The theological suggestions that concluded my consideration of the FAOC report lead to a closing invitation, which illustrates the kind of practical learning that could arise from conversations between church and business communities. Senior Church Leadership is replete with references to the New Testament. I was struck by how few times the Old Testament made an appearance. From my experience of leadership development outside the churches, I highlight three areas where all may learn from the Hebrew tradition.

Wisdom

Despite an emphasis on skills and competence, there has been a welcome rediscovery in recent years of ancient aspects of leadership. John Adair, whom the FAOC report identifies as a pioneer of leadership studies, draws attention to the contribution of Greek philosophers, especially the Aristotelian concept of *phronesis*, practical wisdom.[26] Few leadership courses get far without quoting Lao-Tzu, the founder of Confucianism:

> A leader is best
> When people hardly know he exists
> Not so good when people obey and acclaim him
> Worse when they despise him
> But of a good leader, who talks little,
> When his work is done, his aim fulfilled,
> They will say:
> We did it ourselves.[27]

26 Adair, *How to Grow Leaders*, pp. 50f.

27 Quoted in Richard Bolden et al., *Exploring Leadership: Individual, Organizational and Societal Perspectives*, Oxford: Oxford University Press, 2011, p. 21.

The Hebrew wisdom tradition offers insights well beyond the perennially mistranslated Proverbs 29.18. A correct rendering would be along the lines of 'without a vision, the people lose constraint', a useful text for those involved in change, where the paraphrase, 'run around and do their own thing' may apply. The contemporary relevance of the Hebrew Wisdom tradition in business schools is shown by Phil Jackman.[28]

Narrative

A feature of the Hebrew Bible, as of other ancient texts, is the importance of narrative and storytelling. A leading proponent in this field is Professor Yiannis Gabriel of Bath University's School of Management.[29] Stories can help a community understand itself, perhaps through myths of origins. David Hurst observes that, 'It is the narrative truth contained in history and fiction that explains why so many executives prefer to read novels and biographies rather than management books.'[30]

Covenant

One of the great joys of my work in the overlap of business and faith communities is the discovery of hidden treasures. In this category lies a book by a Professor of Business Ethics: *Leading with Meaning: Using Covenantal Leadership to Build a Better Organisation*. Moses Pava suggests that 'it is more meaningful and pragmatic for leaders to think of organisations ... as being less like machines than like covenants, shared agreements among equal

---

28 Phil Jackman, 'The Contemporary Relevance of the Hebrew Wisdom Tradition', in Chris Mabey and Wolfgang Mayrhofer (eds), *Developing Leadership: Questions Business Schools Don't Ask*, London: Sage, 2015, pp. 231–44. Jackman works for the Agapé Workplace Initiative, www.awi.org.uk.

29 See www.organizational-storytelling.org.uk.

30 David K. Hurst, *The New Ecology of Leadership: Business Mastery in a Chaotic World*, New York, NY: Columbia University Press, 2012, p. 6.

partners.'[31] While theologians may debate the extent to which the partners of the biblical covenant were equal, it is more difficult to challenge Pava's contention that '*Hesed* [steadfast love] is the glue that holds covenants together.'[32] While it may not be appropriate to introduce *hesed* in all leadership development courses, I find that participants understand the importance of relentless consistency (in word and deed, in large and small things).

Towards Conclusions, and Beyond

We began with an insight into improvisation from the world of theatre. I hope my reflection on the FAOC report has provided glimpses of shared meaning that can emerge when people join together and respond to one another. We saw Gary Hamel's plea for theologians to join in the conversation. My hope is that leadership scholars and theologians can meet to explore the paradox highlighted by Preben Friis of being skilled, yet spontaneous, of knowing and not knowing simultaneously.[33] Therein lies a fruit of faithful improvisation.

---

31 Moses Pava, *Leading with Meaning: Using Covenantal Leadership to Build a Better Organization*, New York, NY: Palgrave, 2003, p. xiv.

32 Pava, *Leading with Meaning*, p. 5.

33 Peter Simpson and Hugh Burnard, 'Leaders Achieving Focus in the Place of Not Knowing', *Leadership and Organization Development Journal* 21.5 (2000), pp. 235–42.

3.3 Postscript: Leadership Within[1]

Rachel Treweek

In five minutes I can only offer you a tiny scattering of my thoughts, and so I've chosen to use the word 'within' as a peg.

There's a tiny line in the FAOC report which says 'language is never neutral', and as a former Speech and Language therapist I'd like that writ large. In fact, alongside 'faithful improvisation' I would like to add 'curious interpretation'. Continuing the music analogy, 'curious interpretation' would be along the lines of me as a leader being curious about what people have *actually* heard rather than assuming what I've conveyed; as well as checking out what I have heard in the music of others.

But let me return to that word 'within'. 'With' is at the core of my calling as a leader. It's relational and reflects the connectedness intrinsic to God's creation and who we are created to be in relation to God and each other. I am called to leadership from within the Body of Christ, to exercise my leadership among Christ's followers as we participate with each other in God's mission.

Collaborative leadership for me is about both the 'with' and the 'in' of *amidst*. And that's not shying away from responsibility, hiding behind others or failing to take up authority: distinctiveness of role is not in conflict with collaboration. It's the image of the Body: the eye cannot say to the hand, 'I don't need you.'

---

1 This brief oral reflection was part of a discussion on the Senior Church Leadership report at the College of Bishops meeting in September 2015. We are grateful to Bishop Rachel for permission to quote it here.

Collaborative leadership also ensures I put myself in a place of accountability. I think that sometimes 'collaborative' is confused with 'consensual'. My collaborative leadership won't always be consensual. But it is my responsibility to hold the big picture and not to be blind to the sinews of connections from within which I am speaking or acting.

My blindness to that connectedness is often revealed when conflicts arise from a failure in communication. My leadership means taking responsibility for what needs to be communicated to whom ... and if something isn't communicated then I need to have ensured that that is an intentional decision rather than a consequence of my blindness to the connections of the big picture.

Another reflection is that leadership centred on 'with' means *me* asking who is around me, both visibly when I'm upfront, but also in different places of vision setting and decision taking. Do those around me reflect the diversity of the Body of Christ? Do they enable me to see differently so that I'm not simply living in a comfort zone?

Which brings me to another point. It is stating the obvious perhaps, but what is within me shapes who I am and therefore how I exercise my leadership, and I know it's dangerous if I fail to give attention to my inner landscape. I also know my heart within needs to stay fleshy. Every time I make the transition to a new leadership role the temptation has been to toughen up. Yet each time I have heard God's call to nurture a heart of flesh: staying vulnerable and being open to hurt as well as joy.

Over the years I've reflected much on how I take up my God-given authority whilst also growing in servant leadership. It's about my inner self – *within*. John 13.3 has become very important for me: 'Jesus knowing that the Father had given all things into his hands ... knowing that he had come from God and was going back to God, rose from supper.' Jesus takes the towel knowing who he is; only then does he stand up, take up his authority, and intentionally kneel. Ongoing attention to my inner landscape must be a priority.

One final brief comment about discipleship: The FAOC report poses the leadership question: 'What is needed for the mission and ministry of the Church to flourish?' yet as a bishop I want to be wary of what we mean by that. My focus is the flourishing of God's *Kingdom* and God's transformation. A flourishing church is about God's people sent out to be Church among the people and places of their lives. Disciples and ambassadors for Christ. This is actually what lay ministry is. And if we are committed to forming disciples then we have to look at our culture. In the Diocese of Gloucester I'm going to try and ask those who see themselves as part of the Church to introduce themselves to me by saying something about who they are in relation to their week. Perhaps to tell me that they are a mother or a doctor or a cleaner, or a grandparent, or a volunteer, or ... And only then to tell me that they are also a church warden or a children's leader or a member of a particular worshipping community. It will be interesting to see how this goes.

So in summary: Leading from within, connected *with*, and in relationship with; paying attention to my inner self *within*; and strengthening the followers of Christ to *be sent out*. A scattering of reflections!